The Story of Football in 100 Objects

The Story of Football in 100 Objects

Photographs by Jon Shard[1]

Contents

	Introduction: Football Matters	8
	Timeline	11
1.	Samurai warriors watch Kemari football, 794	12
2.	Ball used in Ashbourne Royal Shrovetide Football match, 1800	14
3.	FA Minute Book, 1863–1875	16
4.	'The Girls of the Period: Playing football,' *Harper's Bazaar*, 28 August 1869	18
5.	Harrow football team photograph, 1871	20
6.	Arnold Kirke Smith's England shirt, 1872	24
7.	East Lancashire Charity Cup trophy, 1882	26
8.	Baines Card of Arthur Wharton, c. 1886–1896	28
9.	Original Football League trophy, 1891	30
10.	British Ladies' FC kit, 1895	32
11.	Eastville Rovers season ticket, 1897–98	36
12.	*Boys' Realm*, 1908	38
13.	Sir Thomas Lipton Trophy winners' medal presented to West Auckland, 1909	40
14.	Alfred Morton's caricature of Colin Veitch of Newcastle United, 1909	42
15.	'The World's Delight': Seaside football game, c. 1912	44
16.	Players' Union armband, 1910	48
17.	FA Cup trophy, 1896	50
18.	Commemorative booklet for Olympic football tournament, 1912	52
19.	Footballers' Battalion recruiting poster, 1915	54
20.	Donald Simpson Bell's Victoria Cross, 1916	56
21.	Portsmouth Ladies photograph, 1917	58
22.	Cigarette case presented to Albert Edward Manns by Bath Ladies AFC, 1922	62

23.	*Fémina Sport* pennant, 1921	65
24.	Lily Bridgett's English Ladies Football Association Challenge Cup winners' medal, 1922	68
25.	Wembley Stadium turnstile, 1923	70
26.	Jack Leslie maquette, 1925	74
27.	Argentinian ball from first half of World Cup final, 1930	77
28.	Germany v England match programme, 1938	80
29.	Chelsea FC programme for British Army v Royal Air Force, 26 April 1943	83
30.	Photograph of Margaret 'Peggy' Melling, Bolton Ladies FC, c. 1946	86
31.	'Saturday Taxpayers' by Gerald Cains, 1953	88
32.	Billy Wright's copy of 'La bohème' by Puccini, 1949	90
33.	FA Amateur Cup	92
34.	Stanley Matthews' FA Cup final kit, 1953	94
35.	Referee Richard Maddison's photo album, 1949–1953	98
36.	Tom Finney's Football Writers' Association Footballer of the Year Award	102
37.	Gift given to Manchester United by Red Star Belgrade the night before the Munich Air Disaster, 1958	105
38.	Margaret Shepherd's Manchester Corinthians shirt, 1958	108
39.	Tony Collins' FA Preliminary Coaching Certificate, 1959	111
40.	Elizabeth Taylor's cardigan, 1962	114
41.	Sheffield Wednesday seat cushion, 1960s	116
42.	Official replica Jules Rimet World Cup trophy, 1966	120
43.	Sir Geoff Hurst's World Cup final shirt, 1966	122
44.	World Cup final ball, 1966	126
45.	Knitted World Cup Willie, 1966	128
46.	George Best's Ballon D'Or, 1968	130

47.	Subbuteo, 1970s	*133*
48.	Gill Sayell's Copa 71 Women's World Cup kitbag, 1971	*136*
49.	Sue Lopez's WFA Mitre Challenge Trophy winners' cup, 1971	*138*
50.	Jack Charlton's FA Cup final Leeds United tracksuit jacket, 1972	*140*
51.	Liz Deighan's England cap, 1974	*144*
52.	Viv Anderson's European Cup medal, 1979	*146*
53.	Photograph of Carol Thomas as England win the Mundialito, 1985	*148*
54.	Leeds Supporters Against Nazis pin-badge, 1988	*152*
55.	Liverpool scarf, 1989	*154*
56.	Gurnam Singh's referee shirt, 1989	*156*
57.	Justin Fashanu *Gay Times* cover, 1991	*160*
58.	Paul Gascoigne's Spitting Image puppet, 1990	*162*
59.	Wembley Stadium seats, 1990	*164*
60.	Replica Premier League trophy, 1992	*168*
61.	FA Premier League press release, 1992	*171*
62.	Hackney Women's FC pennant, 1992	*175*
63.	Jürgen Klinsmann's shirt, 1994	*178*
64.	Ian Wright's Arsenal FC shirt, 1994	*180*
65.	Fantasy Football League sofa, 1994	*182*
66.	Photograph by Chris Unger of England v Nigeria, 1995	*186*
67.	Championship Manager, 1996–97	*188*
68.	Robbie Fowler's FA Cup final Armani suit, 1996	*190*
69.	'Looking Up Sunderland v Coventry City' by Stuart Roy Clarke, 1996	*192*
70.	*Fly Me To The Moon*, Middlesbrough fanzine, 1997	*196*
71.	Denis Irwin's shirt, 1999	*199*
72.	Women's World Cup fan drum	*202*
73.	*Daily Telegraph* Fantasy Football supplement, 1999–2000 season	*204*
74.	ITV Digital Monkey, 2001	*208*
75.	Steve Johnson's England cap	*210*

76.	Fara Williams FA promotional card, Women's Euros, 2005	*212*
77.	Eni Aluko's England shirt, 2007	*214*
78.	Hope Powell's Women's Euros medal, 2009	*216*
79.	Amy Fearn's referee's kit, 2010	*218*
80.	John Motson's sheepskin coat, 2012	*220*
81.	Casey Stoney's GB Olympics football shirt, 2012	*223*
82.	Alistair Patrick-Heselton's headguard, London Paralympics 2012	*226*
83.	Manchester United's Hillsborough tribute tracksuit, 2012	*228*
84.	Portsmouth FC poppy shirt, 2014	*231*
85.	3D model of Sergio Aguero's head, 2015	*234*
86.	Stephen Daley's England shirt, 2019	*236*
87.	Lucy Clark's FA referee shirt, 2018	*238*
88.	'Unity' the inflatable unicorn, 2022	*240*
89.	Lily Parr statue, 2019	*242*
90.	Rashford 1 Boris 0 banner, 2020	*244*
91.	Trent Alexander-Arnold's Black Lives Matter boots, 2020	*246*
92.	Steph Houghton's Manchester City shirt, 2021	*248*
93.	European Super League protest placards, 2021	*250*
94.	Harry Kane's rainbow captain's armband, 2020	*254*
95.	Marine v Tottenham Hotspur ticket, 2021	*256*
96.	Programmes marking the death of Queen Elizabeth II, 2022	*258*
97.	Ellen White's boots, 2022	*262*
98.	Nikita Parris's Euros medal, 2022	*266*
99.	Mary Earps's WSL Manchester United shirt, 2022	*268*
100.	Leah Williamson's Finalissima England shorts, 2023	*270*
101.	Pickles' collar, 1966	*272*

Epilogue: What the National Football Museum does and why	*274*
Acknowledgements	*277*
Endnotes	*278*

Introduction

Football Matters

This book seeks to tell the story of football, the world's most popular and engaging sport, through objects that have been collected through its rich history. Ranging from World Cup final footballs to the world's oldest international shirt, from protest banners to inflatable unicorns, and from opera LPs to knitted cardigans, we have picked out 100 objects – plus a very special 101st – from the National Football Museum's Football Heritage Collection. Each one tells a unique story, not just about the game but about the clubs, players and fans that have shaped the history of the sport. And, together, they reflect a diverse and inclusive vision of the national game.

Founded in 1995, at one of the 'homes of football', Preston, Lancashire, and opened in 2001 at Preston North End's Deepdale Stadium, the National Football Museum set out to explore football's development, from the birth of association football in 1863 to its subsequent global popularity. Since 2012, the museum, which is an independent charity, has been based in Manchester city centre's iconic Urbis building. The Football Heritage Collection is today the world's largest collection of football objects and archives and spans the history of football from its early origins to the present day. It features around 40,000 objects, with around 2,500 on display at the museum at any one time, and includes art, fan memorabilia, toys and games, ceramics, film, photography, trophies, kit, oral histories and archives. The museum includes several permanent collections, such as the FIFA-Langton Collection, along with loans from organisations like the Football Association and The Players Foundation, as well as from major private collectors such as the Priory Collection and the Neville Evans Collection.

The museum's galleries and temporary exhibitions span four floors, using powerful storytelling to highlight football's impact on society and our lives. Visitors can immerse themselves in playful, creative experiences that explore the history of the national game and why football matters to so many people. Highlights

The National Football Museum exists because football matters, and it's through the objects and stories told in this book that the game comes alive.

include the original laws of the game, the 1863 FA Minute Book, the 1966 World Cup Collection, and a penalty shoot-out interactive game which gives visitors the chance to test their skills and score a winner through a goal taken from the original Wembley Stadium. The museum's temporary exhibition programme has explored topics as diverse as computer games, fine art, England's 1966 World Cup triumph on home soil, women's football, the First World War, and the contribution of people of Black heritage to the game.

This book chronicles not just the history of football, but also the history of the National Football Museum and its collection. Early collecting focused on the defining moments, players and matches from the men's game, such as the 1966 World Cup win and the early history of the FA Cup, and the displays in the museum showcased the boots, balls and match-worn shirts from these moments. More recently, however, the museum has sought to redress the balance to better represent the women's game, striving for 50:50 male and female representation across the museum's Hall of Fame and wider content.

Choosing just 100 of the 40,000 items that make up the Football Heritage Collection was no small task, but we hope we've achieved a fairly representative snapshot. Striving to tell the whole story, the book explores not just the player and the clubs, but the fans' stories too. The National Football Museum exists because football matters, and it's through the objects and stories told in this book that the game comes alive.

Timeline

1863 The Football Association is founded in London.

1872 First official international game between Scotland and England and the first English FA Cup final.

1888 Foundation of the Football League.

1904 FIFA is founded.

1921 The English FA bans its clubs from hosting women's games.

1930 The first FIFA Men's World Cup is won by hosts Uruguay.

1954 UEFA is founded.

1966 England host and win the FIFA Men's World Cup.

1969 The English Women's Football Association is founded.

1971 The English FA ends its ban on women's football.

1971 The English Women's Football Association holds its first WFA Cup final.

1972 The first official England women's international is played against Scotland.

1984 The first UEFA Women's European Championship is held. Sweden beat England in the final.

1989 The Hillsborough disaster – 97 Liverpool fans die due to failures by the police and stadium management.

1991 The first FIFA Women's World Cup is held in China and won by the USA. The FA Women's National League is founded.

1992 The English Premier League is founded.

1993 The Women's Football Association merges with the FA.

2011 The FA Women's Super League is founded.

2022 England host and win the UEFA Women's European Championship.

1. Samurai warriors watch Kemari football, *794*

Games similar to football have been played all over the world for hundreds of years. Cultures and societies throughout the world have used ball games for leisure and entertainment as well as a form of exercise, or social interaction. The historical evolution of ball games through to association football – the organised, rule-based, modern football we know today – is long and fascinating.

Cuju, a ball game developed in China c. 210 BC, is often considered as the earliest form of football. Cuju was a competitive team game with a leather ball that had to be kicked through a small hole in a net. It was employed in military training and its influence can be seen in later variations of the game in other Asian countries.

Il Calcio, a sixteenth-century game played in Florence during festivals and public events, was highly physical, often turning violent, and was played with a larger ball that could both be kicked and held. It was revived in the 1930s, widely played in streets and squares using handmade balls of cloth. Three games are still played in Florence every year in June.

Malaysia's Sepak takraw, still played widely today, goes back to the 16th century too. It is played with a rattan ball that is hit over a net at the opposition using feet, head, knees and chest.

This artwork, a woodblock print by Japanese artist Toyohara Chikanobu (1838–1912) is part of the series 'Chiyoda Outer Palace' showing scenes of the shogun, the military ruler of Japan, and his noblemen at Edo Castle, also known as 'Chiyoda Castle'. Chikanobu was one of the leading woodblock print artists in Japan in the Meiji era at the end of the 19th century, and he produced hundreds of print designs of a number of different scenes and subjects. This triptych series consists of 32

'Cuju, a ball game developed in China c.210 BC, is often considered as the earliest form of football.'

12   THE STORY OF FOOTBALL IN 100 OBJECTS

artworks and follows a series of 40 paintings of the 'Chiyoda Inner Palace' and gives a rare insight into life in and around the palace. Chikanobu employed several high-quality printing design techniques such as embossing and burnishing, making the surface smoother and almost shiny.

Here, his subjects engage in activities such as hunting, exercise, martial arts, ceremonies and rituals, and in this picture they perform a Kemari ceremony. The game involves two players kicking a ball back and forth, trying to keep it from hitting the ground, while a third player acts as referee. The ball, known as a mari, would classically be made of deerskin and the game would be played on a court about six or seven meters squared. Here the players are watched by a group of Samurai warriors. There is lovely detail in the artwork with the ball depicted in the air above them, cherry blossom trees framing the scene and the Samurai sitting on the side, sheltered by blue and white striped textile panels. The game of Kemari is thought to have been influenced by Cuju and is still played today on special occasions in Shinto shrines.

Believe it or not, American President George H. W. Bush played the game on an official visit to Japan.

Ball used in Ashbourne Royal Shrovetide Football match, *1800*

2.

Medieval ball games, also sometimes referred to as folk, mob or Shrovetide football, are regarded as one of the ancestors of modern football. These local, informal games, played in villages and towns, were chaotic and had no rules. They involved unlimited numbers of players on opposing teams trying to move a ball to markers at each end of a town, resulting in large masses of people moving from one end of the town to the other, using any means possible to move or drag an inflated pig's bladder. The two sides were often called 'Uppies' and 'Downies' depending on which side of the town they were from or had an allegiance to.

Early references to the game all simply use the terms 'ball play' or 'playing at ball', indicating that the game was not necessarily played exclusively with the feet. By the late Middle Ages many different ball games were played all over the British Isles at Shrovetide, Eastertide and Christmastide. The games stopped being popular in the first half of the nineteenth century when the 1835 Highways Act banned football being played on public highways. Nevertheless, some are still being played today.

The Ba' Game ('ba' being short for 'ball') is a version of medieval football played in Scotland, primarily in Orkney and the Scottish Borders around Christmas and New Year. Ba' games are still played annually in places such as Kirkwall, Orkney, Duns, Scottish Borders, Jedburgh, south of Edinburgh, and Scone, Perth and Kinross, among others.

The Uppies and Downies game is a version of the Ba' game and takes place in Workington, West Cumbria, at Easter. The modern tradition of the game began sometime in the latter half of the nineteenth century and the annual tradition now raises money for local charities.

This ball is from the Royal Shrovetide Football match in Ashbourne, Derbyshire. It is a large stuffed leather ball, hand-painted in bright colours and inscribed 'Ashbourne Royal Shrovetide Football'. The Ashbourne tradition probably started in the 1660s, but its exact origin is unknown as the earliest records were destroyed in a fire in the 1890s. Recent research has shown a possible link to the French game of La Soule, which is played in the town of Tricot, Picardy, on the first Sunday of Lent and Easter Monday. Both bear an image of three cockerels in their heraldic designs.

The Ashbourne game is played over two days. It is legal to kick, carry and throw the ball. The ball is not often kicked but is instead carried through the town by a sequence of 'hugs', similar to a scrum in rugby, involving dozens or even hundreds of people. There are two goalposts roughly three miles apart and a goal is scored when the ball is hit against the scoring posts, two millstones, three successive times. The game is played with no limit to numbers of players or the terrain. Shops in the town are boarded up for the duration of the game.

'The Minute Book's early pages chart how 11 clubs and schools responded to an advert in *Bell's Life in London & Sporting Chronicle* that called for a meeting "for the purpose of promoting the adoption of a general code of rules for football".'

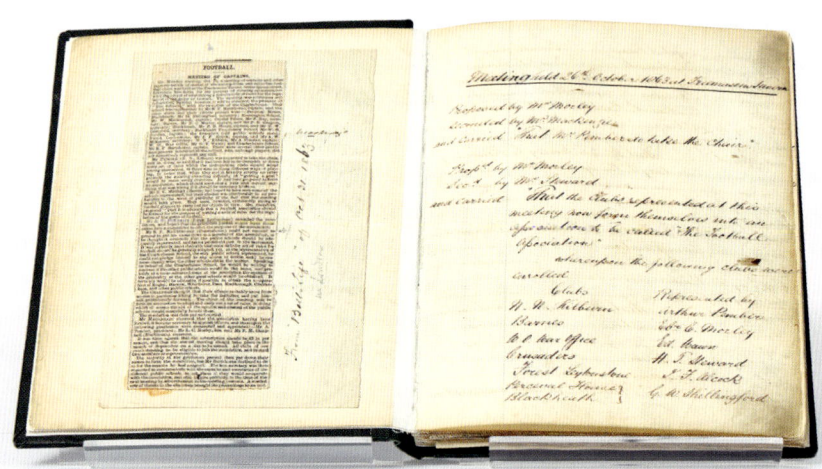

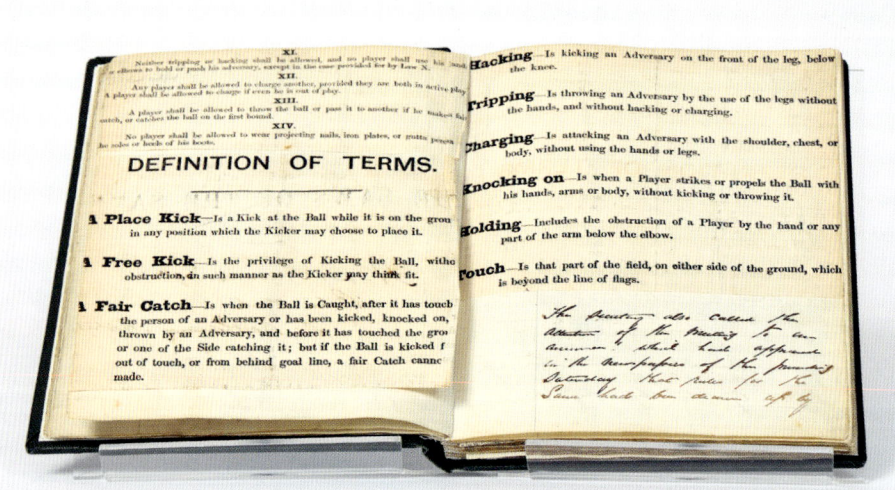

FA Minute Book, *1863-1875*

3.

'In the history of sport, few organisations have begun so unsuccessfully as the Football Association (FA). Its original goal of uniting all football clubs under one code of rules was a complete failure. Just four years after its formation, even its own members considered winding it up. And for the first decade of its own existence, it played second fiddle to rugby football. This was not an auspicious start for what would become the world game.' Tony Collins, sports historian [2]

Given Association Football's modern popularity, it would be easy to assume that its success was predestined. But this FA Minute Book records the opposite.[3] This was not the first attempt to create a uniform code: in 1856 the Cambridge University Football Club printed a code based on various school rules. But they did not catch on, with schools and clubs continuing to use their own.

The Minute Book's early pages chart how 11 clubs and schools responded to an advert in *Bell's Life in London & Sporting Chronicle* that called for a meeting 'for the purpose of promoting the adoption of a general code of rules for football'.[4] When they met on 26 October 1863 at the Freemason's Tavern in London, they founded the FA. Charterhouse, the only public school to attend the meeting, refused to join.

Such was the difficulty in creating a uniform code for the game that numerous meetings were required. Some of the initial proposed laws conflicted with each other and at one point delegates voted for both their own draft and a new code from the University of Cambridge. The laws of the game that were created in 1863 bore relatively little similarity to the modern game, utilising tries, rouges and the catching of the ball by any player. The eventual removal of 'hacking' (the deliberate kicking of an opponent, for those who have never played the game) prompted Blackheath FC to resign, only five weeks after becoming founder members of the FA. Blackheath later went onto become of the founders of the Rugby Football Union.

For a while, the FA's fortunes plummeted. Its membership in 1867 was just 10 clubs, down from 19 in December 1863, and consideration was given to shutting down.[5] But it hung on and soon benefited from the game's rising popularity. In part, this was due to matters outside of the FA's control. Scotland, and Sheffield in England, both had their own thriving football cultures which contributed to the rise and spread of football generally.

But the Minute Book also records two key developments that set the FA onto its rise to prominence. The first was a series of international games, culminating in the first officially recognised game between Scotland and England in 1872. The second came when the FA approved Charles Alcock's proposal that 'a Challenge Cup should be established … for which all clubs should be invited to compete'.[6]

4. 'The Girls of the Period: Playing Football,' *Harper's Bazaar*, 28 August 1869

'This illustration suggests "kick-abouts" or "pick-up" games could involve girls and women as well as men and boys at this time.'

Jean Williams, women's football historian [7]

The American fashion magazine *Harper's Bazar* (later renamed *Harper's Bazaar*) was first published in November 1867. Initially it focused on society news, women's concerns and literature, often reporting on fashion and society trends. On 28 August 1869 the magazine included an illustration of young women kicking a football and enjoying some form of kickabout. For an image such as this to appear in a popular magazine of the period suggests that women kicking a football was not an uncommon sight in the United States.

The illustration shown here was part of a set of four on the page, all beginning with the caption 'The Girls of the Period' and then subtitled with the activity they were doing. For this image the subtitle was 'playing ball', while the other images were of further leisure activities including bathing, rowing and fishing. No other commentary was given, and the illustrations were not linked to another article or story.

> **'For an image such as this to appear in a popular magazine of the period suggests that women kicking a football was not an uncommon sight in the United States.'**

Other sporting activities are captured in this illustration, including a game of women's cricket and women climbing poles (pole climbing was often performed at folk festivals in the States during this period). The women are well-dressed, adding another dimension to the debate about what *Harper's* was aiming to signify with this illustration. Was it capturing a change in society? What does it actually mean?

Those researching the origins of football constantly look for clues like these to help shape an understanding of what football was like during the 1860s. British newspaper articles of the period often talk of children playing football and occasionally of boys playing. Does the difference mean anything? If a report talks of children, should we assume this was a mixed group? It is impossible to say, but we do know that women were participating in forms of football during the formative years of the establishment of governing bodies, such as the Football Association in 1863.

In America, women participated in various forms of football, with the *Detroit Free Press* reporting in 1874 that Vassar College allowed women to play.[8] Four years later the *National Police Gazette* discussed footballing activity in Brooklyn and in Manhattan's Central Park.[9] In 1882 the *Fort Wayne Sentinel* described games played by the West End Ladies' FC, including the kicking of a rubber ball.[10] The lack of detail makes it impossible to identify whether these were association football games or something more akin to American Football. Historian Brian Bunk has written that the earliest known women's game using association football rules in the States was played on 3 December 1893 in San Francisco. He also comments that: 'women in the United States had been playing various types of football since before the country was founded'.[11]

Women's football has often been excluded by mainstream publications, but research by a variety of academics has identified that the natural act of kicking a ball was something participated in by people, regardless of gender, throughout the development of football in the nineteenth century.

5. Harrow football team photograph, *1871*

'By the late 1850s, clubs were formed in England with the sole purpose of playing football. Many began in the London area where, in the autumn of 1863, the Football Association held its first meetings. The people behind the capital's upsurge of interest came mainly from the four major public schools in and around London – Eton, Westminster, Harrow and Charterhouse – and former pupils of these institutions were prominent in establishing the local subculture ... members of these early London clubs were the architects of the form of the game which became known as Association Football.'

Graham Curry, historian [12]

This photograph of Harrow's football team in 1871 was taken at a time when the rules of association football were still developing. Public schools developed their own version of football with rules often created to take into consideration various local factors, for example the placing of a wall, a tree and a door added to the development of the Eton Wall Game – a popular version of the sport still played at the school today.

At Harrow, football was first mentioned in an 1814 school diary, and the oldest surviving rules were drawn up in 1858.[13]

As many public schools developed their own versions of football, it was difficult to organise matches between them. In addition, when students continued their education at university, the lack of a consistent set of rules added difficulties to those trying to organise games. At the University of Cambridge, rules were established in 1848 to try to resolve these issues. Elsewhere in the country other local rules were established, most notably in Sheffield, where a thriving football community developed, at the end of the 1850s.

In 1863 a group of London clubs met and established the Football Association with the aim of creating one unified set of regulations. These became known as the London Rules for several years, as multiple rules for association football still remained despite the establishment of the FA Cup in 1871. In 1877 the FA incorporated a number of Sheffield Rules into its own regulations, and this ultimately meant that one unified set of laws was accepted for the leading competitions of the period.

Those same laws for the game have, in essence, survived. Today there are 17 laws, covering the key aspects (field of play, the ball, players, players' equipment, referees, other match officials, match duration, start/restart of play, the ball in and out of play, determining the outcome of a match, offside, fouls/misconduct, free kicks, penalties, throw-ins, goal kick and corner kick) with several rules and directions within each law.

Despite the unified rules, many of the public schools have retained their own specific games and rules for their own competitions. As with folk games, such as that played on Shrove Tuesday at Ashbourne, the history and heritage associated with the games mean these remain important to those who participate. They do also provide wonderful examples of how games evolve.

A football match report for 'Wanderers v Harrow School', published in *Bell's Life in London* on 11 February 1871, highlights a goalless fixture which featured several Harrow players who went on to play in significant games. These include Walter Paton, who played for the University of Oxford in the 1873 FA Cup final, and Reginald Welch, who became an England international.[14] Their opponents included Charles W Alcock, a Harrow pupil during the 1850s, who became FA secretary in 1870 and was responsible for guiding the game through the establishment of internationals, the FA Cup, the unification of the rules in 1877 and the introduction of professionalism. He remained in that role until 1895, by which time there was a professional Football League of two divisions and multiple competitions around the country and abroad utilising the unified set of laws established.

'At Harrow, football was first mentioned in an 1814 school diary, and the oldest surviving rules were drawn up in 1858.'

Arnold Kirke Smith's England shirt, *1872*

6.

This woollen England international football shirt, worn by Arnold Kirke Smith in 1872, stands as the oldest known football jersey in existence. While it may look drastically different from today's high-tech, sleek football shirts, it remains unmistakably an England kit, proudly displaying the iconic Three Lions badge and crown. Back in those days, football shirts lacked numbers on the back, but the jersey does feature an interesting diamond pattern across the chest, adding a distinct touch to its design.

Kirke Smith was born in April 1850 in Sheffield and attended University College Oxford from 1869. He played as a centre-forward for the university team and represented Scotland in two friendly international matches in 1871. These early matches helped shape the future of international football, although they were not considered official at the time and sometimes drew players from English clubs with Scottish connections.

In 1872, Kirke Smith earned a place in the first official international football match ever played between England and Scotland. This historic event took place on 30 November 1872 at the West of Scotland Cricket Ground in Hamilton. Kirke Smith was one of three players from Oxford University AFC who participated, along with teammates Chapell and Ottaway, the latter of whom was the captain for this game. According to a match report from *The Scotsman* on 2 December 1872, '[t]*he English uniform consisted of white jerseys, with the arms of England as a badge, dark blue caps, and white trousers and knickerbockers. Dark blue jerseys, with the Scottish lion for a badge, white knickerbockers, blue and white striped stockings, and red cowls completed the Scottish uniform.*'[15] Notably, the only surviving item from this historic kit is the England shirt.

The match itself ended in a 0–0 draw, in front of about 4,000 spectators. *The Scotsman* report noted the game was competitive, with 'Scotland having the best of it in the first half of the game, England in the second.'[16] Despite the draw, the game marked a momentous occasion in football history, being the first official international match between two countries.

For Kirke Smith, this match remained his only official appearance for the England national team. However, his football career continued to be notable. In 1873, he captained the University of Oxford team to the FA Cup final, where they faced the Wanderers, the previous season's champions. Unfortunately, the university team lost 2–0.

After leaving Oxford, Kirke Smith pursued a career in the church, eventually taking holy orders. In 1875, he was ordained as a deacon, and the following year he became a priest. He spent the majority of his clerical career in the diocese of Ely. Kirke Smith married and had five children. His family eventually settled in Boxworth, where he served as vicar for 38 years, remaining in the position until his death in 1927. Despite his footballing fame, Kirke Smith's later life was defined by his dedication to the church and his work in the community.

7. East Lancashire Charity Cup trophy, 1882

'It was impossible for a game so popular as that of football to exist many seasons in East Lancashire and charity not to have a share in its bounty. The amount of money taken at almost all big matches has in the aggregate reached a high figure indeed, but as yet no properly organised charity has been made to play a part in the winter game.'

Blackburn Standard, 27 May 1882

During the 1870s and 1880s, association football developed at a rapid rate with clubs appearing across the country. Much of this growth is attributed to the establishment of cup competitions. Competing for a trophy added an impetus and provided a means to measure success. In East Lancashire numerous cup competitions were founded and these gave visibility to the game, encouraging clubs and further tournaments to be established. East Lancashire became a footballing hotbed and by 1882, when this charity cup was created, the Lancashire Football Association was one of the strongest in the game.

There had been some criticism of football becoming a business and this charitable tournament was established as a means of demonstrating that the sport could be used to raise money for positive purposes. In Blackburn the concept of creating the competition proved popular and this ornate trophy was purchased for £156 (equivalent to more than £15,000 in 2025). Blackburn Rovers, Blackburn Olympic, Darwen and Accrington all agreed to compete for the trophy, designed by a Mr W. S. Varley for Blackburn jeweller James Whittle. Olympic went on to win the competition which was, unusually, played during the summer. They defeated Blackburn Rovers 5–2 in a final played before more than 2,000 at Ewood Park.

An article in the *Blackburn Times* on 20 May 1882 talked of the new trophy's design, highlighting that it contained a football scene, a view of Blackburn Infirmary, Lancashire roses and a wreath of leaves for the names of the winning teams.[17] Figures on the base were said to show footballers, with one taking a throw-in and another with the ball at his feet for the kick-off. The coat of arms of Blackburn, Darwen, Accrington and Burnley appear at the base, while surmounted on the handles are figures of a lion (to symbolise strength) and a greyhound (for speed) to demonstrate characteristics footballers needed to have. Below the handles are two heads, one representing William Pilkington, the founder of Blackburn Infirmary.

Charity cups became established in most prominent footballing conurbations as the sport grew and in 1908 the Charity Shield, now the Community Shield, was established to provide a national demonstration of football's ability to raise money for good causes.

Baines Card of Arthur Wharton, c. 1886-1896

8.

John Baines (1958–1908) was the most successful manufacturer of collectable sports cards in the late nineteenth century. He was based in Bradford, as was another key producer, W.N. Sharpe Ltd. Hundreds of different designs have survived and it seems likely that they were first produced to exploit the popularity of rugby in the 1880s.

The cards were sold in bags of six, an approach adopted by many card manufacturers ever since, such as Match Attax. According to Horace Hird, who wrote a contemporary account, the machines that printed the cards were placed near windows so 'it was a familiar sight to see boys peering through … watching the brightly-coloured cards being printed in their thousands — a truly fascinating experience.' While adult fans may have worn the cards as decorations in their clothes for cup ties, the main market was young boys. Baines cleverly encouraged the return of his product by promising prizes such as footballs for the boy who returned the most cards or who collected special gold sets. The latter has echoes of the special wrappers issued by Willy Wonka in Roald Dahl's *Charlie and the Chocolate Factory* (1964). Boys also created a whole subculture of games around the cards, which often involved gambling them against each other.

'Baines promised prizes such as footballs for the boy who returned the most cards or who collected special gold sets.'

While many cards had abstract designs, others depicted individual players, contributing to the rise of the star player in Victorian football culture. The two cards here depict one of the first Black players in English football: Arthur Wharton (*if we look closely, we can see that Arthur is depicted wearing normal clothes as opposed to a football shirt*). While he was not the first Black player outright in the UK (that honour belongs to Andrew Watson, who represented Scotland three times in the early 1880s), Wharton was the first Black player in the English Football League, playing for seven clubs between 1885 and 1902. Born in what is now modern-day Ghana, his father was a Grenadian Missionary of Scottish and West African heritage, while his mother was a member of Fante royalty.

Wharton initially moved to England to become a missionary but soon focused on sport. As well as being an admired goalkeeper, he was a noted runner. One of the cards records that he was the Amateur Athletics Association 100-yard champion, a title he won in 1886 when he equalled the world-record time of ten seconds.

Retiring in 1902, Wharton subsequently worked as a coalminer in Yorkshire. Having developed a drinking problem, he was buried in a pauper's grave when he died in 1930. Since the 1990s the historian Phil Vasili has brought his story into the mainstream and, in 2003, he was inducted to the National Football Museum's Hall of Fame. In 2014 a statue of him was unveiled at England training centre at St George's Park in Staffordshire.

9. Original Football League trophy, *1891*

After the Football Association legalised professional football in 1885, leading clubs now faced the challenges of generating revenue. For several seasons they continued as before, with a mixture of cup games and friendly matches. But these could be one-sided, and friendlies were prone to be being cancelled by one of the teams seeking a better game elsewhere.

In response, 12 Lancashire and midland clubs came together in 1888 to form the Football League, a format which would guarantee reliable fixtures and ensure a certain level of quality control. The initiative came from Scotsman William McGregor, a committee member of Aston Villa. He claimed that cricket's County Championship provided the inspiration.

Preston North End were the first winners in 1888/89, ahead of Aston Villa, Wolverhampton Wanderers, Blackburn Rovers, Bolton Wanderers, West Bromwich Albion, Accrington, Everton (deemed by some to be lucky to be admitted ahead of Bootle), Burnley, Derby County, Notts County and Stoke. Preston also won the first League and FA Cup 'double' and were dubbed 'The Invincibles' after remaining undefeated all season.

However, Preston never held both trophies, because there wasn't yet one for the Football League. Despite all the planning for the new competition, or perhaps because of it, a trophy was not purchased for several years. At a Football League meeting on 25 February 1890, it was agreed a sub-committee would be appointed to 'consider the advisability of having a trophy to be held by the champions each season'.

Given the prominence of Scottish football at this time, it is perhaps not surprising to find that the trophy was made in Scotland by David Dow, a jeweller and silversmith of 68 Argyle Street, Glasgow. They were suitably proud to take out an advert in the *Scottish Referee*, a leading sports paper, telling people they could come and see it in the shop window before it headed south. The cost of the trophy was £52, 10s: this would equate to approximately £5,700 in 2025.

It is sometimes assumed that Everton were the first club to receive the trophy. However, press reports show that it was first presented to Preston North End, as the reigning champions, at a Football League executive meeting at the Bull and Royal Hotel in Preston on 13 February 1891.

Winners were celebrated with the addition of a small shield bearing their name and record. After the original base became full, another, larger base was added. The names that adorn it reflect the growth of the league, as it became a truly national competition in the twentieth century.

Not only did the Football League inspire imitators across the UK, but also across the world. It is still the world's longest-running league competition

'Nicknamed "The Lady", on account of the figure of the Goddess of Victory which adorns it, from 1892 it became the First Division Trophy, as the Football League expanded its membership.'

10. British Ladies' FC kit, *1895*

'Miss Nettie Honeyball, the secretary of the "British Ladies Football Club", of which Lady Florence Dixie is the president, has been interviewed. "I am (sic) just come back from the ground," said Miss Honeyball, sinking into a rocker. "We have been very hard at work. You see, we practice twice a week, and the girls can never get enough of it though we generally go on from about one o'clock to dusk. It's delightful sport, and every member is enthusiastic. We've had one little trial, and the result was 8 goals to 6. As for the costume, Lady Florence Dixie stipulated before becoming president that she didn't want to see the sport ridiculed with long skirts and balloon shoulders. Practically speaking, we wear blue serge knickers, of the divided skirt pattern, and the teams will be in cardinal: A pale blue blouses [sic] respectively. Then, of course, caps are to be worn, and special boots have to be made. At present we have 26 members, ranging between 15 and 26 years of age, while three are married."'

Hull Daily Mail, 7 January 1895

The British Ladies' Football Club was not the first team of female footballers, but it was one of the most famous examples from the 1800s. There had been well publicised games in 1881 between women's teams dubbed 'England' and 'Scotland', and other matches were mentioned on occasion in the years that followed. In 1894 the British Ladies' team was established with support from some notable figures, including Lady Florence Dixie (the daughter of the Marquess of Queensbury), who acted as club president. Dixie was a champion of women's rights, speaking and writing frequently about the need for equality of the sexes at a time when women did not have the vote, never mind many of the other freedoms that would be taken for granted a century later.

Women playing football may seem like a natural activity today but back in the 1890s some would have seen the staging of games as a challenge and newspaper articles, usually written by men, were often critical. Nevertheless, the British Ladies ensured their activities were visible. Even their clothing, such as that shown here, challenged the establishment by doing away with corsets.

'The British Ladies' Football Club was not the first team of female footballers, but it was one of the most famous examples from the 1800s.'

After a few months training, the British Ladies played their first public game in 1895 when a crowd of more than 10,000 was said to have attended their match at Crouch End, London. The club would split into two teams for games, with matches staged between sides representing the North and South or Blues v Reds, for example.

Between 1895 and 1897 they played around 100 matches across Britain and Ireland in places such as Aberdare, Belfast, Bury, Bristol, Cardiff, Darlington, Douglas, Edinburgh, Glasgow, Ipswich, London, Manchester, Newport, Paisley, Plymouth and West Bromwich. There were few areas of the country that could not have been aware of the club.

It is impossible today to state whether these games of football added focus to campaigns for women's rights or changed minds. What was most important about these matches was that they occurred across the country and could not be ignored. They were certainly reported on, even if the tone of reporting was often dismissive. They gave the women involved opportunities to champion their views, such as in February 1895 when Nettie Honeyball explained in a *Daily Sketch* article: 'I founded the association late last year, with the fixed resolve of proving to the world that women are not the "ornamental and useless" creatures men have pictured. I must confess my convictions on all matters, where the sexes are so widely divided, are all on the side of emancipation, and I look forward to the time when ladies may sit in Parliament and have a voice in the direction of affairs, especially those which concern them most.' [18]

The British Ladies ultimately faded but some of their former members continued to play and promote football into the twentieth century.

'After a few months training, the British Ladies played their first public game in 1895 when a crowd of more than 10,000 was said to have attended their match at Crouch End, London.'

11. Eastville Rovers season ticket, *1897-98*

'There is no club in the West that has either more enthusiastic supporters or officials with a stronger desire and determination to succeed than Bristol Eastville Rovers.'

The Bristol Observer, 16 April 1898

By 1897, when this ticket was purchased, the concept of buying a season ticket was well-established. Football clubs introduced them to encourage regular attendance, while also helping to bring in income at a time when the season's expenditure could be planned. Typically going on sale during the close season, they usually provided a discount on the amount spent by fans attending every home game.

Clubs knew that match results and weather could affect attendance, while supporters saw the opportunity of committing to a season as a means of getting a better deal financially. Over time there would also be some kudos in becoming a season ticket holder. Not only did they guarantee you'd be able to attend every home game but you'd also be first in the queue for big match tickets away from home – and simply being a season ticket holder would prove your loyalty as a fan.

This ticket is for Eastville Rovers, who turned professional at the beginning of the 1897–98 campaign, possibly adding to the need to promote season tickets that year. They also performed a share issue to raise capital and that season they joined the Birmingham and District League, in addition to playing in the Western League. The name was changed to Bristol Eastville Rovers and, in February 1899, the club officially became Bristol Rovers.

Name changes like these demonstrate how the game was developing with ambitious clubs looking to represent, or capitalise on, a city's name rather than a district. During the 1890s and early 1900s, many of the clubs that would later become significant changed their names to represent their town or city, such as Ardwick transitioning into Manchester City; Newton Heath reforming as Manchester United; Small Heath becoming Birmingham (and later Birmingham City) and Pine Villa renaming as Oldham Athletic.

This specific season ticket cost five shillings, the equivalent cost of attending 10 Eastville Rovers games that year. As the club played 22 home league matches in 1897–98, spectators enjoyed a significant discount.

John Dorrell was the lucky fan who bought this ticket, and his family have helped paint a picture of his life. At the time he bought the ticket he was 21 and one of 16 children. He worked as a warehouseman and according to Dorrell's family, he died on 15 April 1938 at the age of 62.

'This specific season ticket cost five shillings, the equivalent cost of attending 10 Eastville Rovers games that year. As the club played 22 home league matches in 1897–98, spectators enjoyed a significant discount.'

12. Boys' Realm, 1908

'It is very satisfactory to be able to take credit for creating a vogue for a type of story that did not exist until one invented it.'

Arthur Steffens Hardy, *The Boys' Realm*, 17 October 1925

Little known today, Arthur Steffens Hardy has a genuine claim to being the father of the fictional football story. While Thomas Hughes was perhaps the first to write a fictional depiction in *Tom Brown's Schooldays* (1857), Hardy was the first to popularise ones set in the world of professional football.[19]

They grew out of the wider boom in boys' story papers in the mid to late-nineteenth century. In response to Victorian 'Penny dreadfuls,' *The Boys' Own Paper* (1879) encouraged a trend towards more wholesome and morally improving fare for young readers.

Among these was *The Boys' Realm* (1902–1929) part of a stable of boys' papers published by the Amalgamated Press. They were cheaper than their more middle-class peers and aimed at a broader audience. Initially, *The Boys' Realm* focused on the same diet of school, war and adventure stories. But in 1905, a football story by A.S. Hardy, timed to accompany the FA Cup final, revealed a huge, untapped enthusiasm for stories set in the contemporary world.[20]

A.S. Hardy was the pen name for Arthur Joseph Steffens (1878–1939), who later married the actress Dido Drake. Born to a German father and an English mother, he anglicised his name as a stage actor in comedies and drama. Persuaded to take up writing by friend, he spent the rest of his life working for a variety of boys' papers.

One of his earliest and most successful inventions was the Blue Crusaders team. Several key characters bore striking resemblances to contemporary stars. Silward Harborough was modelled on Vivian Woodward, a striker for Tottenham, Chelsea, England and Great Britain at two Olympics. William Foulke was based on William 'Fatty' Foulke, a substantial and charismatic goalkeeper whose party piece was to pull the crossbar down.

Hardy's success was based in how he blended 'hard facts and imagination', as one editor put it.[21] His heroes and villains reflected wider tropes of boys' literature, but also those of the football world — villainous directors trying to exploit clubs for financial gain, criminals seeking to corrupt players, and egotistical stars.

Most poignant are those tales written during the First World War, when Hardy and his fellow writers reflected both contemporary patriotism and debates and criticism about football's place in wartime society. Hardy's fictional heroes imitated their real-life counterparts by joining a Footballers' Battalion. The adventures that Hardy conjured up appear fantastical, but they were rooted in the world that his readers lived in.

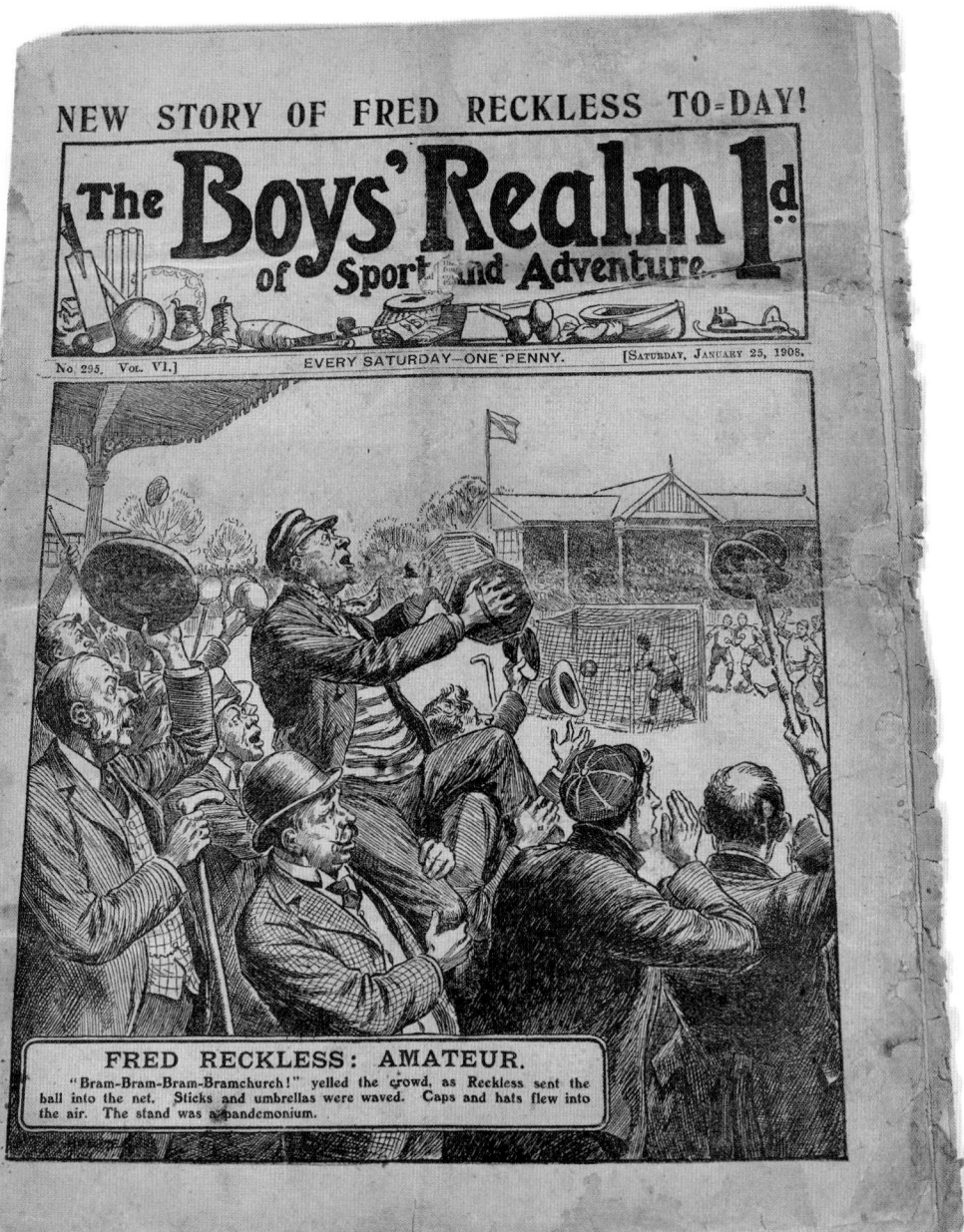

13. Sir Thomas Lipton Trophy winners' medal presented to West Auckland, *1909*

This early football medal tells the extraordinary story of West Auckland FC's visit to Italy in 1909 to take part in the Sir Thomas Lipton Trophy tournament – an international competition between West Auckland as well as clubs from Italy, Germany and Switzerland, and seen as one of the forerunners of the World Cup. How did a team of mostly miners from County Durham get picked to represent England in the first 'World Cup'?

The Sir Thomas Lipton Trophy was first held in 1909 and is related to the Torneo Internazionale *Stampa Sportiva*, organised by sports magazine *La Stampa Sportiva* the previous year. Teams from Italy, France, Germany and Switzerland took part in the earlier

competition, which was deemed a success by the Italian football authorities, but they nevertheless felt it was not a truly international tournament without the participation of an English side. British industrialist Thomas Lipton agreed and donated the Sir Thomas Lipton Trophy, promising to attract an English club for the tournament the following year.

How a humble amateur team ended up being chosen for the tournament is unknown. Italy, Germany and Switzerland sent their finest teams at the time, but the English FA refused to nominate a club. Italian reports from the time suggest that Lipton wanted a side from the Northern League to take part and the team might have been confused with the more prominent and successful Bishop Auckland. Another theory is that West Auckland was confused with Woolwich Arsenal, who dominated the domestic game at the time, sharing the same initials 'W' and 'A'.

Whatever it was that got West Auckland FC onto the invite list, the players took up the challenge with determination and self-belief. Some of them had to fundraise and borrow money to be able to make the trip, pawning furniture and even wedding rings! They travelled to Piedmont in April 1909 and beat Turin FC in the first round to reach the final, where they faced reigning Swiss champions Winterthur. West Auckland won the decider 2–0 and returned home triumphant winners of the first 'World Cup'.

Each player received a medal like this one given to the midfielder Tom Gill. The award is inscribed with 'Torneo Internazionale Football Stampa Sportiva' and '1909' on one side and features a football scene on the reverse.

West Auckland travelled to Turin again in 1911 to defend their title, this time meeting Juventus in the final. They famously beat the Italian club 6–1 and won the trophy outright.

It was proudly displayed in West Auckland's Working Men's Club but was sadly stolen in 1994 and never recovered. An exact replica was made and is now at West Auckland FC. The incredible story of the giant-killing miners' team from County Durham being crowned 'world champions' in 1909 was also made into a film in 1994 called *The World Cup: A Captain's Tale* starring Dennis Waterman.

Alfred Morton's caricature of Colin Veitch of Newcastle United, *1909*

14.

This beautiful caricature was drawn in 1909 by Scotsman Alfred Morton, one of many talented artists who worked for Hulton Press in Manchester. While sports photography was emerging in the 1900s, artists still played a key role in depicting events and attracting readers in the booming sports newspaper market. Morton helped popularise star players as professional football attracted new audiences who followed the sport as much through the press as they did by attending games. Morton's picture carries his trademark imp, a mischievous creature who sometimes appeared as a character in his own right.

It would have been printed across the road from the National Football Museum at Hulton's Withy Grove Press, now home to the Printworks entertainment hub. As historian Steve Tate writes, 'Edward Hulton helped create one of the most dynamic newspaper publishing houses in Victorian Britain, a Manchester-based print centre that by 1900 was reckoned to produce almost five million newspapers a week for both national and regional markets.'[22] A self-made man, Hulton created one of the flagship titles of sporting coverage, *Athletic News*. Known as '*The Times*' of sports papers, its editor for many years was James Catton. Less than five foot in height, Catton was known as the 'Mighty Atom' and was an important figure in sports journalism. He improved the standing and public image of both sportswriters and professional footballers, both having been viewed with some disdain in the late nineteenth century.

It was a vision he shared with Colin Veitch, captain of the Newcastle United side that dominated English football in the 1900s, winning three League titles and appearing in five FA Cup finals, although only winning one. From a middle-class background, Veitch was very much an all-round figure. In football he was a tactician, famously helping shape Newcastle's passing game and notorious off-side trap, and a leading trade unionist for the Players' Union. Away from the game, he was a lover of the arts. According to club historian Paul Joannou, he was a 'playwright, producer, conductor and composer' who was a key figure in the Newcastle People's Theatre and member of the Clarion Choir and Newcastle Operatic Society. He was also a journalist during and after his playing career and was once banned from the Newcastle press box for his criticism in the 1930s.[23]

One of his earlier journalistic efforts was to write a series of profiles of fellow players for *Athletic News* for the princely sum of £2 per article. Featuring a Shakespearean quotation and illustrated by one of Morton's caricatures, they appeared under the penname of 'Polyphemus',[24] with readers invited to guess his identity. Thousands wrote in and around 100 were successful. They included his Magpies teammate Peter McWilliam, who sussed what Veitch was up to after McWilliam appeared in one of the articles. 'His descriptive detailed account of my "peculiarities" leaves me in no doubt as to Colin's identity.'[25]

15. 'The World's Delight': Seaside football game, c. 1912

'But when Stiffy's between the sticks, when Stiffy's between the sticks,

He can stop any kind of football – a football or a brandy ball,

And Vivian Woodward says, when I start my monkey tricks,

"What's the good of me trying to score, when Stiffy's between the sticks?"'

Chorus of 'Stiffy the Goalkeeper,' c. 1912

In its heyday, this seaside game entertained holidaymakers and released the cash from their pockets at Blackpool's famous Pleasure Beach. A photograph exists of the game's promoter, holding out a football as he attempts to tempt passing tourists into trying their skill and luck.[26] For a penny, holidaymakers attempted to kick a football through holes or to knock over figures of famous players. Heavy and mounted on powerful springs, it wouldn't have been easy to win the three penny prizes on offer!

One figure wasn't a player but would have been equally recognisable to any music-hall fan. Before television and radio, music halls were the most popular ways of enjoying popular music and comedy, with many football fans heading to them after a game on a Saturday afternoon. In the centre is a figure of a clown – 'Stiffy the Goalkeeper'. He was the invention of the Liverpool comedian Harry Weldon. Inept and drunk, Stiffy was a comic anti-hero who sang about conceding 62 goals in a game. He was the main character in a sketch called 'The Football Match' where crooks attempted to bribe Stiffy. One villain was played by a young Charlie Chaplin, who later became one of biggest film stars in Hollywood. Adding to fun for the audience was stage prop depicting the crowd at the game – famous players would poke their heads through to represent the watching fans in a form of celebrity cameo.[27]

A game mixing football and music-hall references at one of Britain's most popular seaside holiday resorts encapsulates how association football had travelled from its folk and public school roots to part of the modern mass entertainment industry. Its popularity meant that it increasingly gained civic approval, with politicians and community leaders attending leading games.

In 1914 the game received the ultimate seal of approval when Lord Derby persuaded King George V to attend the FA Cup final for the first time. The winning captain who received the trophy from him is depicted in the metal figure on a standalone base. Tommy Boyle was the commanding centre-half and captain of the Barnsley side that came within a

'Before television and radio, music halls were the most popular ways of enjoying popular music and comedy, with many football fans heading to them after a game on a Saturday afternoon.'

whisker of winning the FA Cup in 1910. After a big-money move to Burnley, he led them to victory in 1914. Boyle was reported to have looked overawed when receiving the trophy and later in life he would write, 'I have a faint impression of a pair of kindly eyes and a charming smile as I looked to take the cup. A great moment in any man's life and yet I can hardly tell you what it was like. Probably you can understand my feelings.' [28] A few months after Boyle's historic achievement, Britain declared war on Germany and joined what became known as the First World War.

Players' Union armband, *1910*

16.

'The Union badges were worn on the field in an English Cup tie. The badges worn in that match were metal and were fastened on the breast. They were unsuitable, hence the present cloth armband.'

Bolton Evening News, 3 September 1910

There had been a trade union for football players in the 1890s. It had been established with the aim of challenging the restriction of movement between clubs and the imposition of a maximum wage of £4 per week, but it had failed. However, footballers remained concerned with both conditions and pay. Billy Meredith, one of the game's biggest stars, had seen a couple of his fellow teammates die while still on the books at Manchester City in 1902 and he was concerned about the support their families received. In addition, Meredith and many of his colleagues were suspended from the game for a significant period of time a few years later, causing him to feel he was a mere pawn at the hands of football's governing bodies.

In December 1907, after he had joined Manchester United, ongoing concern with the way footballers were treated caused him and Charlie Roberts, another leading footballer, to look at establishing a union. They organised a meeting at the Imperial Hotel in Manchester with the intention to challenge the maximum wage and the restriction on transfers. The Players' Union was born.

After initially recognising the Players' Union, the Football Association banned players affiliated to the organisation prior to the 1909–10 season. Some players left the union, but many remained, most notably at Manchester United. When a group of union players, predominantly from United, met and trained together during their ban, they were photographed behind a hurriedly created sign reading: 'The Outcasts F.C.' This highlighted the players' plight, and the union seemed to gain new impetus, especially when Everton footballer Tim Coleman publicly came out in support.[29]

Members of the union were encouraged to wear metal badges to show their support but armbands, such as the one shown here, were more suitable and worn from 1910. Nevertheless, the Football League and FA still objected to players publicising their membership in this way during matches.

Over the following decade, membership increased to around 300 in 1915 and more than 1,000 by 1920. Many battles were won on behalf of players as the union developed, becoming known as the Professional Footballers' Association in 1956. In the 1980s the union set up its Football in the Community initiative, which established community-focused programmes connected with League clubs.

17. FA Cup trophy, *1896*

This beautiful silver trophy is the oldest surviving FA Cup, used between 1896 and 1910. It is an exact replica of the original, which had been in use since the FA Cup's inception in 1871/72. The intricate design features a footballer on the lid and four oval cartouches with the names of the winning teams from that period. The body has two silver-shielded plaques and is 16 inches tall, with a domed base on a wooden plinth.

The FA Cup, the oldest cup competition in the world, was initially made by Martin, Hall & Co in Sheffield and presented to the first winners in 1872, Wanderers, a London team of former public schoolboys. It is often referred to as the 'little tin idol'. Aston Villa had won the FA Cup for the second time in 1895 and proudly paraded the trophy around Birmingham for celebrations. After a few months the cup was exhibited in the display window of a shop owned by local shoe and boot manufacturer and long-time Villa supporter William Shillcock. However, in September 1895, the trophy was stolen overnight from the shop window and never recovered.

A replica of the first trophy was made by Vaughtons in Birmingham and the first team to be presented with this new trophy was The Wednesday (now Sheffield Wednesday) in 1896. Until 1910 when the trophy was withdrawn, it was won by 11 teams, with four of them winning it twice: Aston Villa, Bury, Sheffield United and The Wednesday. Tottenham Hotspur secured it in 1901 and became the last non-league side to clinch the trophy (Spurs entered the Football League in 1908–09). Manchester City won it in 1904 and Manchester United followed suit in 1909 after entering the competition for the first time.

After several unofficial duplicates were made and sold due to not holding the copyright to the design, the FA decided to withdraw the trophy following Newcastle United's victory in 1910. It was presented to Lord Kinnaird to commemorate his twenty-first anniversary as president of the FA. The new, larger trophy was made by Fattorini & Sons in Bradford and presented to the 1911 FA Cup winners, incidentally Bradford City!

The trophy pictured remained in the Kinnaird family for a long time until it was sold at auction in 2005 and bought by the then chairman of Birmingham City, David Gold. It was loaned to the National Football Museum for display for the next 15 years. In 2020 it went back to auction and was acquired by Manchester City's owner, His Highness Sheikh Mansour bin Zayed. The Citizens had been the first club from Manchester to lift the FA Cup when they beat Bolton Wanderers in the 1904 final. After the acquisition, Manchester City Chairman Khaldoon Al Mubaraksaid: 'This cup is a visible reminder of the rich and long history of English football to which Manchester City is inextricably entwined. Winning this actual trophy in 1904 was a turning point for the club and for the city of Manchester in that it firmly cemented football in the heart of its community.'

18. Commemorative booklet for Olympic football tournament, *1912*

'English footballers attach insufficient importance to Olympic football, believing the matches to be little short of a walk-over for the English team. In reality they are nothing of the kind.'

Derby Daily Telegraph, 5 July 1912

This souvenir booklet was one of 24 guides to the results of the 1912 Stockholm Olympics.[30] It was the fifth Olympiad to be held after Frenchman Baron Pierre de Coubertin founded the modern Olympic Games in 1894. At the London Olympics in 1908, Great Britain won what is officially recognised by FIFA as the first Olympic football tournament, with earlier competitions involving club and other unofficial sides. England overcame Denmark 2–0 in the 1908 final and then beat them again, 4–2, to retain their title four years later. This was the high point of British Olympic football success.[31]

Nominally a British side, the team was in fact all English. The Scottish, Irish and Welsh governing bodies turned down the opportunity to participate, so the English FA selected the players. They were all amateurs, as were the other seven competing sides, who were all from Europe. GB beat Hungary 7–0 and Finland 4–0 to reach the final. Against the Finns,

'Woodward was among several members of the British side who served in the armed forces during the First World War.'

captain Vivian Woodward instructed Arthur Egerton Knight to deliberately miss a penalty after disagreeing with the referee's decision to award it. The final was attended by 25,000 spectators, including the Swedish royal family. The Crown Prince chatted with both teams at half-time and when the winners came to collect their medals, forward Harold Walden returned the informality by saying 'thanks King' as he received his.[32]

The star of the Great Britain side in both 1908 and 1912 was team captain and centre-forward Woodward. An architect by profession, he played in the Football League for Tottenham Hotspur and Chelsea, as well as his amateur club of Chelmsford. At international level he scored 29 goals in 23 games for the full England side, 46 in 30 for the amateurs, and five in six for Great Britain. A delicate, skilful player, he also exemplified

the amateur ideal of valuing sportsmanship over victory. Notably, in 1915, he turned down the chance of appearing in the FA Cup final to avoid taking the place of a player who had appeared more regularly for Chelsea.

Woodward was among several members of the British side who served in the armed forces during the First World War. Among them was schoolteacher Joseph Dines, who was killed by a sniper on 27 September 1918. Also to die young was goalkeeper Ronald Brebner, who we see in the cover photograph. He sadly died in 1914 due to injuries sustained while playing for Leicester Fosse.

This brochure captures the high point for Great Britain's football team at the Olympics. When they returned in 1920, they were beaten 3–1 in the first round by Norway. That tournament was won by Belgium in another all-European affair. But in Paris in 1924, Uruguay's victory announced South America's arrival on the global stage.

19. Footballers' Battalion recruiting poster, *1915*

'A call was made for recruits. Parker, the Clapton Orient captain, at once responded amid loud cheers, and he was quickly followed by F. Buckley, of Bradford, the international half-back, Needham, and other members of the Brighton team followed. Altogether thirty-five recruits came forward, including ten Orient players, and were sworn in.'

Sporting Chronicle, 16 December 1914

On 14 December 1914, at Fulham Town Hall, the first recruits for the new Footballers' Battalion (17th Middlesex Regiment) stepped forward. Having listened to speeches urging them to join up, including one by the FA's President, Lord Arthur Kinnaird, who had already lost one son serving with the British Army, they stepped forward to serve King and country.[33]

The 1st Footballers' Battalion was one of the many 'Pals' battalions raised in 1914 and 1915. Britain was the only major power to start the war without a mass army, and the idea of serving with your 'Pals' was used to encourage men to volunteer. The idea is credited to Lord Derby, who had earlier encouraged King George V to become the first reigning monarch to attend an FA Cup final in 1914. Whole battalions were formed around cities, towns, education, jobs and even sports. That a battalion could be formed from football players and fans shows how far the game had become embedded in British life.

The battalion, and this recruiting poster, were also part of the bitter debate about football's place and contribution to the war effort. Professional football controversially continued during the 1914–15 season, attracting abuse from an anti-football campaign backed by much of the right-wing press. Many within football were angered by the attacks and responded by highlighting the game's wider contribution to the war effort and pointing to its own patriotic response. The battalion was founded by the Conservative MP William Joynson-Hicks as criticism of the game peaked in the winter of 1914.

The poster reflects these debates with its choice of images and words. The image of players parading before a crowd reflected the hope that, instead of being held back by supporters, footballers could set an example that would lead them to the frontlines. The quotation from a German newspaper reflected pre-war concerns that Britain's sporting obsession made it, in the words of writer Rudyard Kipling, 'muddied oafs at the goal'.[34] And the exhortation to 'Play the Greater Game on the Field of Honour' echoed the language of the public schools' games ethos, embodied in Sir Henry Newbolt's 1892 poem 'Vitaï Lampada' (The Torch of Life), that saw games as preparations for adult life in service and defence of the British Empire.[35]

By spring 1915 recruiting was complete, with the battalion including some 200 professional players, along with club staff, match officials and fans. In June that year a second battalion (23rd Middlesex Regiment) was formed. The 17th Middlesex served in France from November 1915 until February 1918, when it was disbanded as the Army reorganised. Of the estimated 4,500 who served in its ranks, around 900 were killed.[36] Among them were two of the 35 men who responded to that first call for service in 1914: William Jonas and Richard McFadden of Clapton Orient.

Donald Simpson Bell's Victoria Cross, *1916*

20.

'I must confess that it was the biggest fluke alive and I did nothing ... I chucked the bomb and it did the trick.'

Donald Bell, writing to his mother, 1916 [37]

Temporary Second Lieutenant Donald Simpson Bell downplayed the extent of his actions on the 5 July 1916 when he wrote home. The former schoolteacher and professional footballer had led from the front when, with two other men, he braved enemy fire to destroy a German machine-gun position at the Battle of the Somme. For this action, Bell was recommended for the Victoria Cross, Britain's highest award for military gallantry.[38]

Measuring 35mm wide and 41mm high, the medal is made from bronze cannon captured from the Russia army during the Crimean War (1854–56). The award was created in 1856 by Queen Victoria and was the first open to all ranks. Until 1940 it was Britain's highest award for gallantry and only 1,358 have been awarded.[39] Formerly displayed at the Green Howards Museum, in 2010 it was sold at auction. It was purchased by the Professional Footballers' Association and has been on display at the National Football Museum since 2012.[40]

Born in Harrogate in 1890, Bell excelled in sports as a child. He grew into a powerful young man, six feet high and weighing 14 stone, with a powerful burst of acceleration. His physical and playing strengths led him to play for several noted amateur clubs before he went to London to train as a teacher. There, he played for Crystal Palace as an amateur before returning to Yorkshire to work at Starbeck Council School. He then played for Newcastle United as an amateur before joining Bradford Park Avenue in 1912. He turned professional with them for the 1913–14 season and the club won promotion to the First Division.

After Britain declared war on Germany in August 1914, Bell was one of the first professional players to voluntarily enlist. He was quickly promoted through the ranks, joining the 9th Battalion of the Yorkshire Regiment (better known as the Green Howards) as a temporary Second Lieutenant in 1915. It was around this time that he became engaged to his fiancée, Rhoda Bonson. They were married in 1916, a few weeks before Bell returned to the front for the Battle of the Somme.

On the 10 July 1916, five days after his extraordinary act of courage, Bell was killed while making a similar attempt on another gun placement. Rhoda received letters of condolence from many after her husband's death, including from his batman, John Byers. 'The [Company] worshipped him in their simple, whole-hearted way and so they ought, he saved the lot of us from being completely wiped out, by his heroic act ... we have lost the best officer and gentleman that was ever with this battalion.' [41]

The medal was presented to Rhoda by King George V at a private ceremony at Buckingham Palace. She and Donald had only two married days together. Rhoda never remarried.

21. Portsmouth Ladies photograph, *1917*

'Two startling figures, two short but sturdy girls – well, young women – wearing brilliant yellow and black striped jerseys, white knickers, yellow boots – most obvious football boots without high heels – and dainty six-cornered flat caps covering their back hair like bathing caps, all smiles and swing ... they were the first two lady footballers I had ever set eyes upon ... they woke me out of a reverie into the region of sober fact. In the twinkling of an eye, theories, ideas, fancy, suddenly came into concrete realism.'

Bournemouth Guardian, 27 October 1917.

The startled reaction of a middle-aged sportswriter captures something of the shock contemporaries felt when they encountered Portsmouth Ladies FC. One of more than 240 women's teams known to have played between 1915 and 1918, these Portsmouth clerical and munitions workers played at least 28 games before thousands of fans and raised hundreds of pounds for charity. Photographs of them appeared across the country and even in America. Their rapid rise to prominence was one of the most visible signs of the changing place of women in British society during the First World War.

The demands of total war brought women into many workplaces, particularly munitions work, and encouraged them to raise money through charitable action. Women's football, once discouraged, could be accepted as a necessary wartime concession. Portsmouth was not the first to witness such games, though it seems to be at the forefront of a sustained playing scene in 1916. Photos of their matches appeared in the *Daily Mirror* and may have sparked the spread of women's football across the British Isles.

These images, including this one, were taken by Steven Cribb, a local photographer and later a director at Portsmouth FC. This photo, mounted on card, captures them on the 27 October 1917, with their opponents, the men of Cowes FC. More than half their games were against male opponents who often played with their arms tied behind their backs to handicap them. Such games were technically banned by a 1902 FA ruling.

The tall goalkeeper holding a black cat is Elsie Courtney, the club treasurer. After playing several games, the club was formally constituted in December 1916. The President was Mrs Edith Langdon, wife of Councillor Thomas Langdon, and she may be the woman standing to the far left. Langdon, a local businessman, impresario and MC at dances, promoted and organized many of their games. He organised fund-raising fancy dress balls, at which some of the players appeared in their kit. We can see both sets in this photo – nine players wear yellow and black stripes and two the blue shirts gifted to them by Portsmouth FC. Sadly, we don't know whether the club's secretary, Ada Anscombe, is in the photo. She

'Women's football, once discouraged, could be accepted as a necessary wartime concession.'

was only 15 years old when she appeared in her first charity game in 1914. The daughter of a bricklayer, she emerged as the team's star striker, 'chaired' from the ground by her admiring colleagues after scoring a hat-trick in one game.

Like many women's teams, they do not seem to have played after the Armistice of 1918. Once famous, knowledge of Portsmouth Ladies faded over time. Photographs such as these are vital to rediscovering the hidden histories of women's football.

Grandpa with cap on

centre of picture

22. Cigarette case presented to Albert Edward Manns by Bath Ladies AFC., *1922*

'Mr. A.E. Manns, who has been the hon. Secretary since the formation of the club and very keen in promoting its interests, was surprised at being made the recipient of a handsome silver cigarette case from the officers and players, the whole of the names of the members being engraved on it.'

Bath Chronicle and Weekly Gazette, 1 July 1922

This cigarette case was presented on 30 June 1922 to Albert Edward Manns at the Annual Meeting of Bath Ladies A.F.C. They were one of England's estimated 150 women's teams who played between 1919 and December 1921, when the FA banned female participation in the sport. In total, they are known to have played 10 games before at least 70,000

spectators, raising money for charity. One of their most notable fixtures was against the famous Dick, Kerr Ladies FC, played before a crowd of 25–30,000 at Old Trafford. Whereas other teams seem to have been composed of working-class players, Bath Ladies seem to have been a more middle-class team, indicating how the game's popularity was beginning to spread across class boundaries.

The case is particularly special because of the attention paid to the engravings. On the front is a personalised message that translates as 'Beyond duty, old boy' — a testimony to the work that Manns did behind the scenes. Indeed, his family were also involved, with his wife attending games with their four-year-old daughter Beryl, who became the club mascot. She wore a miniature version of the team's kit, a hockey dress worn over a striped shirt, stockings and a beret to cover the hair, all reflective of a more conservative attitude to female sporting attire.

The reverse is also of significance, as it records the names of 24 players and officials. As such, it is a rare physical record of the names of the women and men involved in this pioneering, if short-lived, club. Thanks to the *Bath Chronicle* and *Weekly Gazette*, we can see that many already knew each other as members of Bath Rowing Club and Bath Dolphins Swimming Club. Indeed, team captain Dorothy Hague was at different times captain of all three clubs. Another rower was vice-captain Constance Zillah Rawlings, over six foot in height and thus nicknamed 'Tiny' by her teammates. When she married in 1928, she left the church to a bridal arch of rowing sculls held by her clubmates.[42] The Harrison family was well represented with four sisters – Audley, Mabel, Edie and Dorothy– and the club never played without at least one in the team. They too were keen swimmers, with Edie, Mabel and Dorothy all swimming along the River Avon from weir to weir when just teenagers.[43]

The timing of the case's presentation is particularly poignant. Had it not been for the FA's ban six months earlier, Bath Ladies may well have continued playing before sizeable crowds and helping raise money for charity. Instead, they became one of the many women's teams who struggled to overcome the obstacles placed in their way.

> 'Whereas other teams seem to have been composed of working-class players, Bath Ladies seem to have been a more middle-class team, indicating how the game's popularity was beginning to spread across class boundaries.'

Fémina Sport pennant, *1921*

23.

'A girls' international "soccer" match in London between our own munition workers and the girls of Paris is well within the bounds of possibility', writes a Paris correspondent.

'In Paris a women's sports organisation has been formed, and a team of girls has been trained to play the Association game.'

Evening News, 1 November 1919

Multiple women's football teams sprung up across England during the First World War and the sport continued to develop in its aftermath. Not only did it grow in Britain, but it also developed in continental Europe, with Paris proving something of a hotbed. In 1919 it was claimed there were more than 18 clubs in the French capital, with *Fémina Sport* perhaps the greatest French team of the era.[44] The club included several prominent sports stars amongst their number, including Carmen Pomies. Often regarded as one of the greatest female footballers to ever play the sport, she participated in several tours of Britain with *Fémina Sport*.

This pennant comes from one of *Fémina Sport*'s tours and would have been handed to the opposition captain prior to kick off in the centre of the pitch. It has embroidered figures of female footballers and carries the club's initials and home city.

Fémina players, alongside others from teams *En Avant* and *Les Sportives*, faced Dick, Kerr Ladies, representing England, in 1920 in what was regarded at the time as an England–France international series. Meetings like these added to the status and glamour of the sport. They often gave spectators a good understanding of women's football, with some of the best players of the era on show.

Dick, Kerr and the French team met on five occasions that year and the popularity of these games, together with connections established between the players, ensured further tours followed.

After a spell in England with Dick, Kerr Ladies, Pomies captained *Fémina* and brought them to Britain in 1925 for a 10-match tour, with games played at Belfast, Chorley, Dumfries, Fallowfield (Manchester), Herne Hill (twice), Hyde, Kilmarnock, Mellor, Padiham, By this time the ban on women's football being staged at FA-affiliated clubs was in force but these tour games remained popular attractions.

In a preview for a game in Dore, South Yorkshire, a report in the *Sheffield Independent* (23 July 1932) claimed *Fémina* had been the French champions for seven consecutive seasons without losing a game.[45] Perceived in a similar way to Preston's Dick, Kerr Ladies, *Fémina*

were a force in the women's game, promoting the sport both in France and via tours, such as the ones to England during the 1920s and 1930s. In 1933 they played games against a variety of English clubs, such as York's Terry's ladies team, and these matches were often promoted as England v France.

As well as meetings in Britain, Preston's Dick, Kerr Ladies also travelled to France for tours too, before the Second World War. The subsequent development of women's football owes much to other teams, but throughout the 1920s and 1930s, the touring French sides brought an international feel to women's football in this country.

'Multiple women's football teams sprung up across England during the First World War and the sport continued to develop in its aftermath.'

24. Lily Bridgett's English Ladies Football Association Challenge Cup winners' medal, *1922*

This simple inscription on the back of a small medal, measuring 30mm wide by 35mm high, holds a great wealth of historic significance for the history of women's football in England. It was awarded to Lily Bridgett of Stoke Ladies. On 24 June 1922 they beat Doncaster & Bentley 3–1 at Cobridge in Stoke-on-Trent. She and her teammates were the winners of the first and, until 1970 the only national cup tournament for women's teams in England: The English Ladies Football Association Cup. The ELFA was itself a short-lived attempt to provide a governing body for women's football in defiance of the FA's ban of women's football on association grounds in 1921. Its President was also the manager of Stoke Ladies, Bridgett's father, Leonard Bridgett.

Much of what we know about Stoke and the ELFA comes from the work of historian Patrick Brennan.[46] Through newspaper and family relatives, he has pieced together a history of both organisations. Bridgett was a niece of the famous Stoke, Sunderland and England football Arthur Bridgett. But it was her father Leonard who ran the side alongside a fish and grocery business. Her sisters, Ida and Eva, also played for the team, which was only in existence from 1921 to 1923.

Leonard Bridgett became the ESFA's Chairman on 17 December 1921. Seven days earlier, representatives from around 30 women's clubs attended a meeting in Liverpool in discuss how to defy the FA's ban. They resolved to form the ELFA 'to popularise the game among girls and to assist charity'. However, there was one notable absentee from this meeting and later membership of the ELFA – Dick, Kerr Ladies. It seems most likely that their manager, Alfred Frankland, preferred the touring model that his club undertook, rather than orthodox league and cup competitions.

From the start, the ELFA Cup seems to have struggled in the face of the obstacles raised by the FA's ban. Only 23 of the 58 affiliated clubs entered the competition, with teams perhaps put off by logistical and financial challenges. Results are hard to come by, and it is not entirely clear if all the scheduled games took place. The one organisation willing to help female players was the Northern Rugby Union (today's Rugby League), who allowed its clubs to host games. Heavy rain on the day of the final led to a small crowd of 2,000, but there was consolation for Leonard Bridgett in that Stoke won the trophy which he had purchased for the competition.

There were further highlights for Stoke Ladies. In 1923 they travelled to Barcelona, where they beat *Les Sportives* of Paris to win a trophy offered by the *Cooperativa de Casas Baratas*, an organisation supporting cheap housing. The trophy can be seen on display at the museum thanks to the Neville Evans Collection. The club's final game saw them finally beat Dick, Kerr Ladies 1–0 in 1923. Lily's playing career may have been relatively short, but it encompassed some of the key events in the history of women's football.

Wembley Stadium turnstile, *1923*   25.

This original turnstile from Wembley Stadium, installed in 1923, is one of the larger items in the National Football Museum collection. Before turnstiles were invented, fans entered grounds through simple gates, often rushing through together, creating unsafe conditions and making it difficult to track ticket sales. As crowds grew in the twentieth century, football stadiums and other venues began installing turnstiles to control entry and ensure safety. The introduction of turnstiles allowed only one person to enter at a time, acting as a barrier and regulating access.

Between 1890 and 1960, most turnstiles at football grounds were patented and manufactured by W.T. Ellison of Salford. In 1892, the company patented the 'rush-preventive' turnstile and later added improvements such as a counter to track the number of spectators and prevent entry once the stadium reached capacity. Another key feature was a foot lever that could only be operated by an attendant, allowing controlled passage for each individual. The cast-iron, waist-high design was fully enclosed, preventing people from ducking under and sneaking in without a ticket.

In 1923, W.T. Ellison provided 100 turnstiles for Wembley Stadium. The FA Cup final between Bolton Wanderers and West Ham United was the first event of any kind taking place at Wembley as it was completed ahead of its scheduled opening in 1924. The official capacity of Wembley was 125,000, but estimates suggest that between 150,000 and 300,000 fans gained entry that day, with and without tickets. All seemed calm when gates opened at 11.30am but by 1pm huge crowds of people had gathered all around the stadium, blocking the roads and flooding into the ground. The terraces overflowed and the turnstiles were locked at 1.45pm to prevent more people gaining access. However, the mass of fans still outside rushed at the barriers and forced their way in, climbing over the turnstiles. Inside, fans climbed over fences to prevent being crushed and a large amount of people were standing on and around the pitch.

The situation nearly caused the match to be cancelled, but mounted police were deployed to clear the pitch. The iconic image of the day featured a grey horse named 'Billy', which stood out in the black-and-white footage, leading to the showpiece event being dubbed the 'White Horse Final'. The match, which kicked off 45 minutes late, saw Bolton Wanderers defeat West Ham 2–0. Despite about a thousand fans being injured in the chaos, only 22 required hospital treatment, while two police officers were also hurt.

The chaotic scenes led to debates in Parliament, and recommendations were made to improve safety, including replacing the old turnstiles with newer models and adding extra gates and railings around the stadium. Modern-day turnstiles have evolved significantly, with full-height units in use today. Despite this, W.T. Ellison's designs were a key step in improving crowd control and safety at the time, making them an important part of stadium history.

'W.T. Ellison's designs were a key step in improving crowd control and safety at the time, making them an important part of stadium history.'

Jack Leslie maquette, *1925*

26.

'There was a bit of an uproar in the papers. Folks in the town were very upset. No one ever told me official-like, but that had to be the reason, me Mum was English but me Daddy was Black.'

Jack Leslie [47]

Before Viv Anderson became the England men's first senior Black footballer in 1978, there was another player who could have achieved that feat 53 years earlier. Jack Leslie was born in Canning Town, London, in 1901, to a Black Jamaican father and a white English mother. Between 1919 –1921, Leslie first played for the London League side Barking Town. His prolific scoring record over those two years attracted the attention of Plymouth Argyle.

He made his Plymouth debut in a 0–0 draw to Merthyr Tydfil on 19 November 1921. Leslie was the only Black player in the Football League at that time and remained so for several years, until Eddie Parris arrived at Bradford Park Avenue in 1929. It took time for the talented inside-left to establish himself in manager Bob Jack's starting lineup but, by the end of the 1924 –25 season, Leslie was the club's top scorer with 14 goals.

He and the club started the next season brightly and when the FA International Selection Committee met on 5 October 1925 to select players for the upcoming England match against Ireland, Plymouth were top of the Third Division South and Leslie had scored six goals.

The committee named a squad of 13 players that included 11 starters and two reserves, one of whom was Jack Leslie. The press published his name as a travelling reserve in the squad, and he was called into manager Bob Jack's office to inform him he'd been selected.

However, when the squad travelled to Northern Ireland on 21 October, Leslie was not with them and his place had been taken by Stan Earle of West Ham United. At the time the FA claimed the Plymouth player had never been picked and his inclusion in the press was a mistake.

'Before Viv Anderson became the England men's first senior Black footballer in 1978, there was another player who could have achieved that feat 53 years earlier.'

Years later, Leslie said he felt he had been dropped because of the colour of his skin as FA officials came to have a look at his face and not his football. 'It is not impossible,' said his biographer 'that Leslie was chosen without any knowledge of his colour. Leslie was playing in the Third Division (South) and would not have been very well known.'[48]

During his time at Plymouth, Leslie scored 137 goals in 401 appearances in the third and second tiers, making him the club's fourth-highest goal scorer and ninth-highest record appearance holder.

Decades later, Plymouth fans Matt Tiller and Greg Foxsmith discovered Leslie's story and came together to successfully lead a campaign to build a statue in his honour. His story is powerfully represented in the bronze maquette, which is a scaled version of the statue that was unveiled at Plymouth's Home Park stadium in 2022.

'I hope to create a statue of peerless quality celebrating excellence, that will also represent respect, dignity, devotion and invigorate the quest for equal rights for all,' said sculptor, Andy Edwards.[49]

More recently, Leslie was awarded a posthumous honorary cap in recognition of the adversity he faced due to the colour of his skin.

> 'Jack Leslie was awarded a posthumous honorary cap in recognition of the adversity he faced due to the colour of his skin.'

Argentinian ball from first half of World Cup final, *1930*

27.

'They take their football seriously in South America. Uruguay beat the Argentine in the final of the so-called world's Association football championship at Montevideo by four goals to two, and there followed scenes of great excitement.

'Uruguayans paraded the streets of Buenos Aires, shots were fired, and the police had to disperse the crowd. Later the Argentines held a counter-demonstration and threw stones at the Uruguayan Consulate.

'One hundred thousand people saw the match between Uruguay and the Argentine, and the scenes of enthusiasm on the ground put even an F.A. Cup final in the shade. As a precaution, all the shops in Montevideo were shut.'

Portsmouth Evening News, 1 August 1930

The first men's World Cup tournament was played in 1930 at Uruguay with every country affiliated to FIFA invited to compete. Ultimately, 13 countries participated: Argentina, Belgium, Bolivia, Brazil, Chile, France, Mexico, Paraguay, Peru, Romania, USA, Uruguay and Yugoslavia.

There had been attempts to include England and the other home nations, none of whom were members of FIFA at the time, but they were rejected by each country. Egypt had planned to participate but there was a storm in the Mediterranean and they couldn't travel.

All games were staged in Montevideo, with the concluding matches played at the Estadio Centenario. The hosts faced Argentina in the final after the teams defeated Yugoslavia and the USA respectively in the semis. The final was played on 30 July 1930 in front of an official crowd of 93,000, with an estimated 15,000 travelling from Argentina, but there was controversy pre-match. The two finalists each wanted to use their preferred ball, with the Uruguayans wanting to use a T-Model and the Argentinians preferring a Tiento ball. A compromise was reached whereby a different one would be used in each half, with the pictured ball being the Tiento Argentina selected for the first period.

Using the ball they preferred, Argentina took a 2–1 lead by half-time, though Uruguay's Pablo Dorado was the historic first World Cup final goal scorer. His low shot from the right sent the ball seen here into the net in the 12th minute.

'The first men's World Cup tournament was played in 1930 at Uruguay with every country affiliated to FIFA invited to compete. Ultimately, 13 countries participated'

The Uruguayans took control after the interval, and the final ended 4–2. Their ball should have been used in the second half, but some claim this Argentinian Tiento was used for the full game. According to an article in *When Saturday Comes* in June 2018, photographic evidence appears to back this claim up.[50] Regardless, we do know this ball was the first used in a World Cup final.

The 1930 World Cup received some coverage in Britain, but the media tone was often dismissive. A view held at the time was that the tournament could hardly be described as a World Cup if it didn't include England. The Three Lions first competed in the 1950 World Cup, the fourth such tournament. The first World Cup qualification match staged in England was a 9–2 victory over Ireland at Maine Road, Manchester, on 16 November 1949. Co-incidentally, Uruguay won their second World Cup in 1950.

Since 1950, England have entered every men's World Cup, though they failed to qualify for the Finals in 1974, 1978 and 1994, winning the tournament for the only time in 1966. Prior to the 2026 edition, seven other nations have won the World Cup. They are: Brazil (1958, 1962, 1970, 1994 and 2002), Germany (1954, 1974, 1990 and 2014), Italy (1934, 1938, 1982 and 2006), Argentina (1978, 1986 and 2022), France (1998 and 2018), Uruguay (1930 and 1950) and Spain (2010).

Germany v England match programme, *1938*

28.

'Even to this day, I still feel shame whenever I sit by the fire and glance through my scrapbooks and gaze on that infamous picture of an England team lining up like a bunch of Nazi robots, giving the dreaded salute.'

Stanley Matthews [51]

The most shameful moment in the history of the English international team came on 15 May 1938 when England played Germany. Today, the game is remembered not for England's 6–3 victory, but for the infamous fascist Nazi salute given by the England team at the behest of the British government and the Football Association.

This programme was produced to meet the huge interest in the England team among German spectators, 105,000 of whom watched the game. It reflects the prestige that England still enjoyed, with one article calling them the 'Teachers of Football', while much of the 42-page programme is given over to profiles of the English players. But with a welcome from the German Reichssportführer, it is also revealing of how the Nazi Party utilised sport for political purposes.

The salute represented a remarkable reversal of attitudes towards Germany since the First World War ended. In 1920, England, Scotland, Wales and Ireland left FIFA over the latter's refusal to ban the former Central Powers and any country that played them, and it wasn't until 1930 that England played Germany again in Berlin. When England hosted Germany in 1935, the Nazi party had come to power. The game attracted protests from Jewish, Trade Unions and other anti-fascists, while the German team gave their now customary fascist salute before kick-off. By 1938, the situation was further clouded by fears of war and the British government's policy of appeasement.

> **'Today, the game is remembered not for England's 6-3 victory, but for the infamous fascist Nazi salute given by the England team at the behest of the British government and the Football Association.'**

Spielführer Fritz Szepan,
Hans Jakob
und die anderen Kameraden
von der Nationalmannschaft

It was the British Ambassador to Germany, Sir Neville Henderson, who advised the FA to give the salute. It was felt to be diplomatically prudent and was defended as such by the FA Secretary, Stanley Rous, a veteran of the First World War. He had volunteered in 1914 and seen active service with the Royal Field Artillery, while Charles Wreford-Brown, the FA Councillor in charge of the England party, had lost two brothers and a brother-in-law in the war.[52]

Rous would later claim the players accepted the salute without issue and 'saw it as a bit of fun'.[53] Ascertaining what the players thought at the time is difficult, because few were asked directly. At the time, captain Eddie Hapgood thought that standing to attention was enough and later wrote after the war that he was sickened by the episode.[54] He was followed by others like Cliff Bastin, who spoke of FA threats not to select players who refused the salute. An element of this has morphed into a modern myth on X (formerly Twitter) that claims Stan Cullis was dropped after voicing opposition to the gesture.[55] While he may well have done so, he was never dropped, as his selection as a reserve had been announced weeks in advance. Moreover, Cullis was part of the England side that gave the Italian fascist salute to loud cheers before their game in Rome in 1939.[56]

Chelsea FC programme for British Army v Royal Air Force, *26 April 1943*

29.

Compared to the First World War, the second global conflict of the twentieth century saw the UK Government make greater use of the game in aiding the war effort. The armed forces took sport seriously and the sides that represented the Royal Air Force and the Army at Stamford Bridge on 26 April 1943 were composed entirely of leading professional players, many of whom were internationals in peace or wartime games. These matches were staged to encourage members of the forces generally to play sport, and to foster relationships between allied forces stationed in the UK. They also raised much-needed money for services charities caring for the wounded and their families during and after the war.

Out of the celebrated names, there is one less well-known today but who holds a special place in English football history. Playing out of position at left-half (left midfield) was Leading Aircraftman Frank Soo. Normally, he would play at right-half behind his Stoke City teammate Stanley Matthews.[57] He was the first player of East Asian heritage in the Football League.

> **'Playing out of position at left-half (left midfield) was Leading Aircraftman Frank Soo. Normally, he would play at right-half behind his Stoke City teammate Stanley Matthews. He was the first player of East Asian heritage in the Football League.'**

Soo's father was Quan Soo, who came to Manchester from Guangzhou in China. In 1908 he married his wife, Beatrice, and they ran a laundrette. This was a time of hostility to Chinese immigrants and the family moved to Buxton and later Liverpool. Soo signed for Stoke in 1933 and made 268 appearances in peace and war between then and 1945. He was a popular figure in Stoke-on-Trent, with more than 2,000 fans waiting outside the church when he married in 1938.

During the Second World War, Soo served in the RAF. He was fortunate to be deployed in a ground role but one of his brothers, Ronald, became an Air-Gunner and Navigator in the RAF. He asked to go to China to fight the Japanese, who had been at war with China since 1937, but instead flew with Bomber Command over Europe. In 1944, Ronald Soo and his crew were killed over Brunswick in Germany.

'In 2017 Alan Lau created the Frank Soo Foundation to share his story and Soo was inducted into the National Football Museum Hall of Fame in 2024.'

Soo became the first player of East Asian descent to play for an England representative side. While wartime internationals were not recognised by the FA, due to some players being unavailable for selection because of military service, they were still fiercely competitive and popular fixtures. Soo played nine times for England before crowds of up to 133,000. Seven of the players who were selected for the RAF v Army game shown here appeared alongside Soo for what was probably his highlight for England – a 6–2 win over Scotland at Wembley before 90,000 spectators on 14 October 1944.

Soo later played for Leicester City and Chelmsford Town before becoming a manager. He coached in Italy and Scandinavia, where he managed the Norwegian team at the 1952 Olympics. In 2017 Alan Lau created the Frank Soo Foundation to share his story. After Soo was inducted into the National Football Museum Hall of Fame in 2024, Lau explained, 'It means a lot to us, our communities and also the Soo family. This highlights the positive effect that people from ESEA and Pan-Asian communities have had on football and we hope this will inspire the next generations of boys and girls to aspire to be the next Frank Soo.' [58]

CHELSEA FOOTBALL CLUB

Official Programme

MONDAY APRIL 26th 1943 **PRICE ONE PENNY**

BRITISH ARMY v. ROYAL AIR FORCE

INTER-ALLIED SERVICES Cup Competition Final Tie **Kick-off 3.15 p.m.**

BRITISH ARMY (Red)

S/I. SWIFT, F. V.
Goal

Dvr. CARABINE, J. Pte. COMPTON, L.
Right Back (2) Left Back (3)

C.S.M.I. BRITTON, C. S. S/I. CULLIS, S. C.S.M.I. MERCER, J.
Right Half (4) Centre Half (5) Left Half (6)

Sgt. NELSON, A. Sgt. ROBINSON, J. Sgt. WESTCOTT, D. S/I. HAGAN, J. S/I. COMPTON, D.
Outside Right (7) Inside Right (8) Centre (9) Inside Left (10) Outside Left (11)

Referee—Mr. G. READER (Hants.) Linesmen { Mr. J. WELLER — Red and White Flag
Mr. A. J. WALTER — Blue and White Flag

Sgt. BURBANKS, W. E. Sgt. DOHERTY, P. D. P/O. DRAKE, E. J. Sgt. CARTER, H. Cpl. MATTHEWS, S.
Outside Left (11) Inside Left (10) Centre (9) Inside Right (8) Outside Right (7)

L.A.C. SOO, F. F/Lt. B. JOY L.A.C. BURGESS, R.
Left Half (6) Centre Half (5) Right Half (4)

Sgt. HARDWICK, G. F. Sgt. SCOTT, L.
Left Back (3) Right Back (2)

F/Sgt. MARKS, W. C.
Goal

ROYAL AIR FORCE (Light Blue)

THE INTER-ALLIED SERVICES CUP COMPETITION was inaugurated by The Football Association three years ago with the following objects in view : (1) To encourage Association football among the personnel of the several Allied Forces stationed in this country and to foster international fellowship through our sport, and (2) to raise funds for the Service Charities of those organisations competing in the competition.

The Scheme was warmly received by the Allies and each season has seen an increase in the number of Services which has joined the competition as well as an increased patronage. Each year, too, a larger sum of money has been available to distribute to the charities.

This season, in the First Round, the Fighting French were beaten 1—0 by the Norwegians at Reading, the R.A.F. won their match against the Police and Civil Defence XI at Huddersfield, and the Polish Army were defeated by the British Army team.

The results of the Second Round were : the Belgian Army beat the Czechoslovakian Army, the R.A.F. beat the Royal Netherlands Army, the Army beat the United States Army, and the Norwegian Forces beat the Canadian Army.

Truscotts, London [P.T.O.

30. Photograph of Margaret 'Peggy' Melling, Bolton Ladies FC, *c. 1946*

'Women playing football? Mm! That sounds interesting – and so 10,000 people, mainly men and boys, with a sprinkling of women, found their way to New Meadowbank, Edinburgh, last night, and watched the Bolton Ladies F.C. beat the Edinburgh Lady Dynamos F.C., 6–2. Queues outside the field waited admission a long time after the match had started.'

Unidentified newspaper report, 28 August 1946 [59]

Bolton's reward for beating Edinburgh Lady Dynamos, one of Scotland's top female teams, was to win the Esta Henry Challenge Cup. And we believe it is this cup that Margaret 'Peggy' Melling is proudly holding in this studio photograph.

It is important evidence of women's football during the era of the FA ban. (1921–1971). This harmed the development of the women's game, but it did not erase it. Instead, from the 1920s to the 1960s, females across the country formed teams and played where they could. The best-known team of this era is Dick, Kerr Ladies FC from nearby Preston. The challenge for historians is to uncover and record the stories of other teams.

Thanks to the work of researcher Helga Faller, we know Bolton Ladies played at least 29 games between 1939 and 1952. Not only were they one of the longer-running clubs of this period, but they also played several games billed as international matches, facing sides from Scotland and Wales. One of these in Edinburgh attracted a crowd of between 10,000 and 17,000. They were also filmed for a Pathé newsreel when they played against the Edinburgh Dynamos in Salford in 1946.[60] Like many women's teams, their matches raised money for charity. Amongst those they helped were the people affected by the 1946 Burnden Park stadium disaster, which saw 33 people die and more than 400 injured during an FA Cup tie between Bolton Wanderers and Stoke City.[61]

Melling often played at centre-half, but like many players at this time, she played several positions. Her programmes include handmade notes about the line-ups, including one time she played in goal. The team also included Nellie Halstead, a bronze medallist in the 4 x 100m relay at the 1932 Los Angeles Summer Olympics, and who also played for Dick, Kerr's.[62]

Throughout her life Melling lived in the village of Billinge, which is between Wigan and St Helens in Lancashire. Alongside her football efforts, she and her mother were well known for running a fish and chip shop for many years. A *St Helens Star* article from 2007 describes how, 'Peggy was well known at her little fish-and-chip shop as a person not to be trifled with … although she did have a soft spot for the hard-up and down-at-heel.' The paper described her as a 'tallish woman who always wore men's trousers and was a heavy smoker. She had a puckish sense of humour and also ran a betting shop in the village.'[63]

Melling died in 1990, aged 68. She never married, so her collection of more than 40 items from her playing career went to her niece, Elizabeth Stockley. After her death, her husband Clifford decided that he wanted them to be preserved for future generations by donating it to the museum. It is one of the largest single donations we received relating to women's football before the 1960s.

31. 'Saturday Taxpayers' by Gerald Cains, *1953*

'I had a dream of roughly the painting ... I hadn't been to many other football grounds anyway, only Fratton Park, and I always tended to stand at the open end, because they were cheaper really, and I based it on that.'

Gerald Cains [64]

At 22 years old, Gerald Cains was the youngest artist whose work appeared in the 1953 *Football and the Fine Arts* competition. Organised by the FA to celebrate its 90th anniversary, they and The Arts Council invited artists to compete for prizes totalling near £3,000. The brief was broad, inviting artists to depict 'any aspect of association football, not only the game itself, but all its related activities', and in any of six forms: paintings, drawings, watercolours, engravings, lithographs and sculptures. As historian Ray Physick writes, the competition was most likely the brainchild of the FA Secretary, Sir Stanley Rous, who would have been familiar with arts competitions organised at the London Olympics of 1948.[65]

In 2015, Cains was interviewed by the National Football Museum as part of the Heritage Lottery Fund 'Art of Football' project. They discussed his entry, which had become part of the museum's collections. Called 'Saturday Taxpayers', it depicted Portsmouth FC's Fratton Park stadium. He explained how he created the painting while doing his National Service and classified it as 'social realism'.[66]

Today, perhaps the best-known work from the Football and the Fine Arts exhibition in 1953 is one of the four winners who split the £1,000 painting prize. In 1999, the Professional Footballers' Association spent £1.9 million to buy L.S. Lowry's 'Going to the

'In 1999, the Professional Footballers' Association spent £1.9 million to buy L.S. Lowry's "Going to the Match", a depiction of his trademark "matchstick men" heading to Burnden Park, home of Bolton Wanderers.'

Match', a depiction of his trademark 'matchstick men' heading to Burnden Park, home of Bolton Wanderers. For the PFA's Chief Executive, Gordon Taylor, it represented 'the heart and soul of the game and the anticipation of fans on their way to the ground'. [67]

Cains and Lowry both focused on the most popular topic in the exhibition — stadiums. At least 40 works focus on them. Many others depict games in community scenes such as parks or streets, with portraits of star players a surprisingly small portion overall. The final selection of 156 pieces were exhibited by the International Faculty of Arts at Park Lane House, London, for three weeks, before going on a year-long tour across England and Scotland. It attracted lots of interest from galleries and the public, but some did not feel that football was a suitable subject for art, with one Arts Council representative complaining, 'Three huge rooms full of footballers is too much for anyone, especially in view of some of the horrors included.' [68] In contrast the judges and organisers felt the works were of good quality and that the exhibition was a success. Ray Physick argues that the exhibition was important and pioneering, not only because it took the game to a 'sceptical art world', but also to areas of the population ignored by the art establishment.

32. Billy Wright's copy of 'La bohème' by Puccini, *1949*

'Billy Wright's love of opera dates back to his visit to Italy with the England team two years ago, when he went to see one of the principal Italian opera houses and saw "La bohème". He told Italian newsreel cameramen about it before last year's match against Italy at White Hart Lane, and was surprised to receive a complete recording of the opera by air from Italy a few days later. It was a present from the cameramen.'

Birmingham Gazette, 1 March 1951

Given the weight and size of the gift, it's no wonder that Billy Wright was surprised by the generosity of the Italian cameramen. The album holds 13 records of the opera in its entirety, as performed by the famous La Scala Opera House of Milan. It not only reveals something of Wright's personal life through his love of music, but also how the life and image of the professional footballer was changing in post-war Britain.

Wright was the very essence of the 'model pro', a term used by the historian Joyce Woolridge to describe how the image of the professional footballer became more respectable in the post-1945 period.[69] Player autobiographies, which became popular in the 1950s, were a key part of the process and Wright penned no less than four between 1950 and 1962.[70]

> **'Wright found an equally passionate lover of music in his wife, Joy Beverley, one-third of the Beverley Sisters pop group. They were arguably football and pop music's first celebrity couple when they married in 1959.'**

As captain of the Wolves side that won three First Division titles and the 1949 FA Cup, and the first man to win 100 England caps, he had plenty to say about matters on the pitch. But he often reflected on the perks that came with playing with England abroad, including three World Cups. He appreciated how, in travelling to Brazil for the 1950 World Cup or behind the Iron Curtain to the Soviet Union in 1958, he was seeing the world in a way not possible for most Britons.

Listening to these records would have been a communal activity with his landlady and her family, Mrs Colley. He first joined them as a teenage apprentice on the Wolves ground

staff and remained with them throughout most of his playing career. Photos of Wright with his records show him sat in the family living room, sometimes with Mrs Colley.

Wright found an equally passionate lover of music in his wife, Joy Beverley, one-third of the Beverley Sisters pop group. They were arguably football and pop music's first celebrity couple when they married in 1959.

The album was donated by the late Graham Hughes, who gave more than 40 years of service to Wolverhampton Wanderers.[71] Starting as a handyman, he later worked in ground maintenance before becoming the club's historian. Such was the esteem for Hughes at the club that a stand was named after him in 2003. Friendly with many former Wolves players, especially Steve Bull, Hughes received the album from Wright. This was a characteristically generous gift, with Wright giving away many of his international caps in later years.

FA Amateur Cup

33.

The base of the FA Amateur Cup lists 71 clubs who won the trophy between 1893–94 and 1973–74. The small plaque for 1951 lists a somewhat unusual name – Pegasus. Formed just three years before, Pegasus reflected a longer preoccupation with class and money that shaped English football.[72] The club's prime mover was Dr Harold Thompson of St John's College, Oxford, and later Chairman of the FA. It was created to raise the profile of university football among the public schools and the wider public. Players had to be students at Oxford or Cambridge Universities or to have left the previous year. They were not as callow as might be imagined, with many players in their mid-twenties, having gone to university after service in the armed forces. The club's ambition was wining the FA Amateur Cup, something they achieved twice, in 1951 and 1953.

The FA Amateur Cup was born out of the class divides of nineteenth-century British society. The Victorian middle-classes believed in sport for sports sake, in contrast to a longer working-class tradition of playing for money. While the FA did not split over the issue, as rugby football did in 1895, a separate national cup competition was created in 1892 for amateur clubs. The first winners were old Carthusians, one of only two clubs (the other being Wimbledon) to win both the FA and FA Amateur Cups.

While it was a national competition, its finalists and winners reflected the dominance of two areas: the North-East and South-East of England. After 1911, only four winners came from outside the Northern League, Isthmian League, or Athenian League. The final's heyday as a spectator event was the 1950s. After 60,000 attended the 1948 final at Stamford Bridge, it was switched to Wembley. Thereafter, it always hosted the final, although not any replays. The 1950s saw attendances of up to 100,000 and it was still drawing between 40–50,000 in the 1960s.

These amateur players were not always as pure as the FA wished. Shamateurism existed at both northern and southern clubs. This was the practise of secret payments or other types of benefits to players to encourage them not to turn professional. In the era of the maximum wage (1901–1961), an amateur player with a good job and under-the-counter payments could rival a top-class professional for income. The FA disproved of the practice and in 1927–28, 341 Northern League players and many officials were suspended over illegal payments. It was known as the 'Crook Town affair', after the club exposed how widespread the practice was after a complaint by Bishop Auckland.[73]

The Bishops became the tournament's leading club. They won it 10 times, twice as many any other club, and were losing finalists a further eight times. Between 1955 and 1957 they became the only side to win the final three years in a row. The star of that team was their captain Bob Hardisty, who also captained the Great Britain Olympic football team in 1948, 1952 and 1956. After the Munich Air Crash in 1957, Hardisty came out of retirement to assist Manchester United.

34. Stanley Matthews' FA Cup final kit, *1953*

One of the few examples of a full kit in the National Football Museum collection, this bright tangerine shirt brings back memories of one of the greatest FA Cup finals ever, and Sir Stanley Matthews is regarded by many as one of the best players the game has ever seen.

Matthews was born in 1915 in Stoke-on-Trent. His father was a professional boxer, so sport and competing were in his blood, and he learnt from a young age to train hard to achieve. After playing football for his school team and appearing once for England Schoolboys, Matthews joined Stoke City in 1932, playing on the right wing. His superb passing, dribbling and ball control skills soon earned him the nickname 'Wizard of Dribble'. He made 259 league appearances for Stoke and scored 51 goals, helping Stoke to win the Second Division title in 1933. Matthews made his senior international bow in September 1934 against Wales and scored one of England's four goals that day, becoming the first teenager to score on his debut. He made a further 53 appearances for the Three Lions and represented the RAF throughout the Second World War.

This kit is arguably from Stanley Matthews' most memorable game. Despite an already illustrious career, he joined Blackpool in 1947 and helped lead the team reach FA Cup finals in 1948 and 1951, but both ended in disappointing defeats. He was 38 years old when he appeared in his third FA Cup final in 1953, which was widely considered to be his last chance to win the prestigious competition. Blackpool met Bolton Wanderers in the Wembley showpiece and were 3–1 down with 22 minutes to go. It looked like Blackpool were heading for another defeat when Matthews crossed to Stan Mortensen, whose goal helped ignite a remarkable comeback for the Seasiders. Mortensen's free-kick levelled

'The first-ever winner of the Ballon d'Or in 1956, Matthews was also the inaugural recipient of the Football Writers' Association Footballer of the Year award in 1948.'

'Matthews' superb passing, dribbling and ball control skills soon earned him the nickname "Wizard of Dribble". He made 259 league appearances for Stoke and scored 51 goals, helping Stoke to win the Second Division title in 1933.'

the scores in the 89th minute and then, with seconds left on the clock, William Perry dramatically converted another Matthews cross to give the Seasiders a sensational 4–3 victory. Despite Mortensen becoming the first and only player to have scored an FA Cup final hat-trick at Wembley, the game is commonly referred to as the 'Matthews Final' in tribute to the winger, whose individual brilliance helped Blackpool secure a famous triumph.

Throughout his career, Matthews amassed numerous accolades. In 1965 he became the only footballer to be knighted while still playing. The first-ever winner of the Ballon d'Or in 1956, Matthews was also the inaugural recipient of the Football Writers' Association Footballer of the Year award in 1948. His longevity in the game was unparalleled, as he became the oldest player to play in the top division of English football at 50 years and five days old. Additionally, Matthews set the record as the oldest player to represent England, at the age of 42 years and 142 days. Sir Stanley leaves a legacy as one of English football's greatest players and his iconic moments, including the unforgettable 1953 FA Cup final, remain a testament to his genius on the field.

35. Referee Richard Maddison's photo album, *1949-1953*

'The atmosphere can be overwhelming.'

Richard Maddison

'I'm in the net,' is how referee Richard Maddison laconically captioned one photograph of himself in action. The image in question captures him surrounded by players, officials and policemen, all watched by tens of thousands of Argentinian football fans. Taken during a game at the La Bombonera stadium between Boca Juniors and Racing Club in the Argentinian Primera División on 10 October 1949, it is one of many that Maddison collected during a short but fascinating period when British referees were recruited to South and Central America.[74]

A former miner and soldier in the Army, Maddison was one of about 60 or so British referees who swapped Molineux for the Maracanã and Boundary Park for La Bombonera. While association football had been played in South America since 1867, professionalism came later than in Europe; 1931 in Argentina, and 1933 in Brazil and Chile.

Domestic referees, who were never well regarded, faced immense pressure from spectators, players, officials and the media. After various assaults, disputed decisions and allegations of favouritism toward big clubs, the Argentinian FA sought to improve refereeing standards. In 1937 they recruited a recently retired referee, Isaac Caswell. He appeared for three seasons there before the Second World War disrupted sporting contacts with Europe. In 1948, 14 British referees travelled to Argentina and Brazil. This was the start of a 12-year period which would see British officials also hired in Chile, Colombia, Costa Rica, Mexico, Paraguay, Peru and Uruguay.

Maddison arrived in 1949, a year after 10 referees had been hired by the Argentinian FA. Four did not return, and Maddison himself spent just two seasons in Argentina. At a time when referees were still paid expenses only in England, they received £100 per month (comparable to a top-class player in England), making them some of the earliest professional referees in English football history.

Aside from the money, Maddison's album reveals two of the key attractions. For many, post-war Britain was a grim land of austerity, bitter winters, and fuel and food rationing. The album includes many typical tourist photos but these were opportunities unaffordable to most Britons. Particularly eye-catching for anyone contemplating their limited meat ration at the time would have been Richard's photos of an *asado*, an Argentinian barbecue.

If escaping dreary Britain for South American sunshine and plenty was one attraction, then the other was the chance to experience a football culture that most Europeans knew little about. The late 1940s saw several mega-stadiums constructed in Argentina, aided by President Juan Peron's government. Racing Club even named their new 100,000 capacity ground after him. But while fan disorder was a risk, and some referees were assaulted, Richard and others were deeply impressed by the skill of the South American players and the passion of the supporters.

The pinnacle of Maddison's career came when he was one of five British referees at the 1953 Copa America in Peru. He officiated eight games. In one he was kicked by a player, while another between Chile and Bolivia had to be abandoned after 66 minutes due to unsporting behaviour. In total, Maddison and his colleagues controlled 20 of 22 games, indicative of the prestige of British referees at that time.

After returning to Britain, Maddison spent many years working for Ross Foods in Grimsby. When he retired in 1977, the company magazine interviewed him about his time in South America. He remembered it fondly, although he had a word of warning for the British players heading to the World Cup in Argentina the following year: 'They will rarely, if ever, have experienced anything like the incredibly fanatical support for the South American teams. The atmosphere can be overwhelming.' [75]

> 'A former miner and soldier in the Army, Maddison was one of about 60 or so British referees who swapped Molineux for the Maracanã and Boundary Park for La Bombonera.'

36. Tom Finney's Football Writers' Association Footballer of the Year Award

'Tom Finney thanked his father for being responsible for his becoming a good footballer when he replied to the presentation of the statuette awarded to him as the elected Footballer of the Year at the Press Club last night by Jack Orange, Sports Editor of the Evening News. He said that at a tender age Preston offered him a ground staff job at 50s a week. As an apprentice plumber he was getting 6s a week. He wanted to jump at Preston's offer, but his father advised him to think it over carefully … Tom delayed signing for Preston until he had mastered his job.'

Evening News, 30 April 1954

Over time a multitude of footballing awards were developed to honour individual achievements but in the 1950s there was one main prize to recognise the best player in the domestic season, the Football Writers' Association (FWA) Footballer of the Year Award.

Judged by journalists reporting on football throughout the season, the award was founded in 1947–48. Blackpool's Stanley Matthews was the inaugural winner, and the award has been presented annually ever since. Preston's Tom Finney was the seventh recipient, following Matthews, Johnny Carey (Manchester United), Joe Mercer (Arsenal), Harry Johnston (Blackpool), Billy Wright (Wolverhampton Wanderers) and Nat Lofthouse (Bolton Wanderers).

Finney was an outstanding goalscorer for both Preston and England, earning 76 caps and netting 30 goals. With Preston, his hometown team, he made 473 League and Cup appearances, scoring 210, after joining the club during wartime. As with all players from that era, all wartime domestic and international appearances are not included in competitive statistics and so his figures would be much higher if they were.

'Known as the "Preston Plumber" as he continued his trade, running his own plumbing business alongside playing at the highest level, Finney thrilled crowds wherever he played.'

Known as the 'Preston Plumber' as he continued his trade, running his own plumbing business alongside playing at the highest level, Finney thrilled crowds wherever he played. In 1953–54 he made 31 League appearances, scoring 14 goals, and helped Preston reach the FA Cup final too. He was much in demand by the media throughout the Cup run, writing articles for various newspapers, and could have earned a considerable sum for himself in the days when English football's maximum wage was in force. However, demonstrating a commitment to the team rather than himself, he insisted on any money raised being shared equally between the Preston players.[76]

In 1954 the Player of the Year Award was presented at the FWA dinner on the Thursday night, prior to Saturday's FA Cup final. Preston lost 3–2 against West Bromwich Albion at Wembley and Finney later admitted he thought the FWA dinner affected his preparation and performance, which he felt was not up to his usual standard.

Finney was to make history by becoming the first player to win the FWA award twice. After Manchester City's Don Revie (1955) and Bert Trautmann (1956) were honoured, Finney's second success deservedly came in 1957. Others, including Stanley Matthews, Kenny Dalglish and Cristiano Ronaldo, matched Finney's double success, but the first man to eclipse it was Thierry Henry, who won the award on three occasions (2003, 2004 and 2006).

In 1960, Finney retired from Preston after a persistent problem with a groin injury, but continued to make appearances in charity matches and testimonials. In 1962 he made one appearance for Toronto City in Canada and then, in 1963, he was persuaded to play for Irish club Distillery against Benfica in the European Cup.

Finney died in 2014 at the age of 91, but his name is remembered via a statue outside Deepdale, Preston North End's stadium. He was a major supporter of the National Football Museum.

Gift given to Manchester United by Red Star Belgrade the night before the Munich Air Disaster, *1958*

37.

'The BEA Elizabethan carrying the Manchester United team home from Belgrade crashed on take-off at Munich Airport today ... A BEA spokesman said later it was "understood there were ten to fifteen survivors out of forty people on board. This is not definitely confirmed." The air-liner was reported to have plunged 60ft to the ground. Manchester United team played Jugoslav (sic) Red Star in Belgrade yesterday and drew 3–3. Manchester United are the outstanding club in post-war English soccer and have been League Champions for the past two seasons. United are due to meet Wolverhampton at Old Trafford on Saturday.'

Huddersfield Daily Examiner, 6 February 1958

The plate shown here was presented to the Manchester United players at their European Cup meeting with Red Star Belgrade, played on 5 February 1958. That night United had progressed to the semi-finals of the competition with a team renowned throughout Europe. Known as the Busby Babes, as many of this youthful team had been brought through the club's ranks by manager Matt Busby, this United team was exciting, skilful and hugely successful. The world was shocked when their return flight to England ended in tragedy.

United's plane had stopped for refuelling at Munich. When the flight resumed, two attempts to take-off were abandoned and then the third resulted in a horrific crash. The plane hit slush on the runway, ploughed through a fence and hit a house. The left wing was torn off and then the tail section broke off and hit a barn. Those passengers that could move evacuated the plane, with United goalkeeper Harry Gregg helping pull survivors from the wreckage.

Of the 44 people on board, 23 died. They were:

United players (with their ages in brackets): Geoff Bent (25), Roger Byrne (28), Eddie Colman (21), Duncan Edwards (21), Mark Jones (24), David Pegg (22), Tommy Taylor (26) and Liam 'Billy' Whelan (22).

United staff: Walter Crickmer (club secretary), Tom Curry (trainer) and Bert Whalley (coach).

Journalists: Alf Clarke, Don Davies, George Follows, Tom Jackson, Archie Ledbrooke, Eric Thompson and Frank Swift (former Manchester City and England goalkeeper).

Others: Tom Cable (steward), Bela Miklos (travel agent), Capt Kenneth Rayment (co-pilot) and Willie Satinoff (supporter).

There were 21 survivors, including manager Matt Busby and the following players: Johnny Berry (never played again), Jackie Blanchflower (never played again), Bobby Charlton, Bill Foulkes, Harry Gregg, Ken Morgans, Albert Scanlon, Dennis Viollet and Ray Wood.

The tragedy rocked football and the loss of so many lives, particularly of young, popular footballers, brought emotion across the country. Steve Fleet, who was a reserve goalkeeper with United's great rival City, was the best friend of Eddie Colman and as soon as he heard of the crash he went to Colman's house in Salford. 'None of us had a telephone, so the only way we could find out what was happening was by going to the off-licence down the road and call United,' he recalled. 'I went to do it, called Old Trafford and that's when I was told he'd gone. Les Olive asked me to tell his parents — something you never think you have to do, especially at that age. Eddie was going to be my best man. I couldn't believe he'd gone. Moments like that change your life. They make you realise what's important. I had to go back to the house then and tell Eddie's parents. His dad didn't believe me. He couldn't accept it. He went to the off-licence and made another call. It was awful.' [77]

Disasters devastate communities and this air crash hurt deeply. The plate, photographed here, was recovered from the wreckage and is a powerful reminder of a day when pure joy was soon followed by tragedy.

> 'The tragedy rocked football and the loss of so many lives, particularly of young, popular footballers, brought emotion across the country.'

38. Margaret Shepherd's Manchester Corinthians shirt, *1958*

'We all worked every day, training twice a week, and the team was still brilliant. Imagine if we'd have had all they have today! We'd train on Fog Lane Park but in winter there'd be so much ice or mud it was difficult. We had a little shed where we got changed. No lights in there! If you wanted a wash you'd break the ice on the duck pond. You'd go home muddy sometimes. We did it for the love of football.'

Margaret Shepherd in *Manchester Corinthians: The Authorised History*, 2025

Manchester Corinthian Ladies Football Club was established during the 1948–49 season under founding manager Percy Ashley, whose daughter Doris had been a prominent player with Bolton Ladies.

The Corinthians were not the first Manchester-based women's team, but they were the first to tour extensively promoting women's football across the world at a time when the FA ban was still in force. Initially, they played in charity and friendly matches in Britain, but in 1957 they travelled abroad for the first time, playing in Portugal. Within a little more than a year they had made five trips to the continent, touring Portugal (twice), Germany (twice) and Holland. They had also played games in Madeira in 1958, prior to their second Portugal tour. On each tour they played in major stadia, including Lisbon's Alvalade Stadium, before large attendances.

> **'The Corinthians were not the first Manchester-based women's team, but they were the first to tour extensively promoting women's football across the world at a time when the FA ban was still in force.'**

In Germany they participated in the International Ladies Football Association's (ILFA) European Cup, winning the tournament as an unofficial England team. The ILFA didn't last but that should not detract from the significance of what they achieved as the Corinthians demonstrated that women's football could prove popular on the largest stages.

Further tours followed during the 1960s, including trips to Morocco, Tunisia and Italy, but the greatest success came at the start of the decade when the Corinthians enjoyed

a three-month-long tour of South America and the West Indies. During this trip they participated in and won another international tournament in Venezuela. This was a significant landmark in the history of women's football and added to the sustained success of the Corinthians.

This shirt lists the overseas tours undertaken in 1957–58 and belongs to Margaret Shepherd, who joined the club a decade later. Shepherd participated in another major overseas tournament in 1970 when the Corinthians won a prominent competition in Reims, France, after defeating Juventus 1–0 in the final.

By the time of the Reims success the Corinthians had played a prominent role in the birth of the Women's Football Association (WFA) and its FA Cup competition. Its manager, Gladys Aikin, was a WFA committee member, and she was also the first chair of the WFA's International Committee prior to the first official England women's international in 1972. Aikin also played a significant role in the establishment of women's leagues in the north-west.

Manchester Corinthians played on into the 1990s, with their last trophy success coming in 1989 when they won the Three Counties League.[78] The team finally ceased to exist in 1992 but many of the club's former players played leading roles in the development of other women's teams, including Macclesfield Ladies, Manchester City and Stockport County.

'Manchester Corinthians played on into the 1990s, with their last trophy success coming in 1989 when they won the Three Counties League.'

Tony Collins' FA Preliminary Coaching Certificate, *1959*

39.

'Tony was a true pioneer of the sport. He was known throughout the game for his ability to recognise and nurture talent, a skill which enabled him to have a huge impact on the lives of others.'

Howard Wilkinson, Chairman of the League Managers' Association, 2021 [79]

This simple certificate marks the start of a post-playing career that saw Anthony 'Tony' Norman Collins become the first black manager in the English Football League. Indeed, more than three decades would pass until another followed in his footsteps.

Collins was born in Kensington in London in 1926. His mother was unmarried, and his grandparents helped raise him as a child. He was young enough at the start of the Second World War to be sent away from London due to fears of German bombing. Homesick, he returned to the capital and was signed by Brentford as a junior before he joined the Army in 1944, aged 18. His football exploits while stationed in Italy led to him being recommended to Sheffield Wednesday, who signed him in 1947. He made his Football League debut with York City in 1949, the start of a 12-year playing career that saw him make 333 League appearances for six clubs.

Like a growing number of players at this time, he opted to take an FA coaching course to widen his post-playing opportunities. Originating in the 1930s, these courses really took off in the post-1945 period. For former players, they offered a way to prepare for a post-playing career. For members of the public, such as teachers, they helped prepare them for coaching grass-roots sides, particularly youth teams.

The certificate is signed by the FA's Director of Coaching, Walter Winterbottom. Incredible as it may seem today, this also involved managing the senior England side. Between 1946 and 1962, Winterbottom took England to four World Cup finals, although they never managed to get beyond the last eight. Arguably, his greatest legacy was the development of the FA's coaching programme, personally running many of the courses.

'The certificate is signed by the FA's Director of Coaching, Walter Winterbottom. Incredible as it may seem today, this also involved managing the senior England side.'

THE FOOTBALL ASSOCIATION

Patron: HER MAJESTY THE QUEEN
President: H.R.H. THE DUKE OF EDINBURGH, K.G.

Secretary:
SIR STANLEY ROUS, C.B.E., J.P.

Chairman of Council:
A. DREWRY, ESQ., C.B.E., J.P

PRELIMINARY CERTIFICATE FOR COACHING

Mr A.N. Collins,

has attended a Football Association Course for Coaches and has been examined in the following subjects

1 – PRACTICAL COACHING
2 – PRACTICAL PERFORMANCE
3 – THEORY—COACHING METHOD
4 – THEORY—LAWS OF THE GAME

THIS IS TO CERTIFY that

Mr A.N. Collins,

has satisfied the examiners that he has good knowledge of coaching technique and that he is capable of coaching the fundamentals of the game

CHAIRMAN OF
INSTRUCTIONAL COMMITTEE

DIRECTOR OF COACHING

Collins took the course while he was still playing, and his first move into management saw him combine playing with managerial duties at Rochdale in 1960 and 1961. He then retired and managed the club until 1967. His greatest achievement was taking his Fourth Division club to the 1962 League Cup final, where they lost 4–0 on aggregate to Second Division Norwich City.

After stepping down at Rochdale, he was unable to find another managerial post. Instead, he became a scout, most notably for Don Revie at Leeds United. Collins was key to Revie's meticulous pre-match preparations, providing detailed briefings on rival teams and players that analysed their strengths and weaknesses. One press report dubbed him 'The Master Spy'. When Revie became the England manager in 1974, Collins joined his backroom staff. Later Collins scouted for several major clubs, including Manchester United, until the age of 80.

'Collins' greatest achievement was taking his Fourth Division club to the 1962 League Cup final.'

Elizabeth Taylor's cardigan, *1962* 40.

'Miss Betty Taylor … who celebrates her 20th birthday today, can look back with satisfaction on the past year, for one of her main ambitions – the reformation of the Accrington ladies football team – has now been well and truly realised!'

Newspaper clipping dated 1 May 1962 [80]

This cardigan was worn by Elizabeth 'Betty' Taylor, manager of Accrington Wanderers from 1962 to 1965. It was knitted by club secretary Pat Broderick, who played alongside Taylor as they defied the FA's ban on women's football. The design is of male players from a graph pattern produced by the Canadian company Mary Maxim.[81] The advertising envisaged men wearing it. Instead, Taylor and Broderick wore their cardigans in several photographs taken to promote the team.

The cardigan was loaned to the museum by Taylor with the assistance of her niece, Rachel Robinson, and Trizia Wells of *History in Action*. It was Wells who first promoted Taylor's story as part of the *Women's Work Project*, funded by the National Lottery Heritage Fund. After Taylor's death in 2024, aged 81, Robinson kindly allowed the museum to continue displaying the cardigan.

Elizabeth Taylor was born in 1942 in Clayton-le-Moors, into a wrestling dynasty. Describing herself as 'always a tomboy', Taylor said that she showed early promise as a footballer while still at school.[82] 'The boys used to scream for me when they were picking the teams … all the lads were jealous.' While working at the Accrington Bus Corporation on leaving school she joined Accrington Wanderers, the town's women's team. In 1962, when Margaret Ashworth, the team's player-manager, decided to retire from the team she had led since 1953, she suggested to Taylor that she take over. Taylor was unsure at first, describing herself as a shy 19-year-old, but she soon rose to the challenge.

Taylor led the team through four seasons from 1962 to 1965; each was played during the close season from May to August, so as not to clash with men's games. They used a local farmer's field, and their club rules extended a welcome to players of any age, providing they were 'fit, and big enough, and keen'. Taylor knew how to use the local press, keeping the club profile high with a mixed match against a boys' Sea Cadets team, and arranging for the Mayor of Accrington to kick off in a game against Nelson Ladies.

They also made the news when they challenged the FA's ban in 1962. FA Secretary Denis Fellows' sympathetic, if cautious, reply survives in her collection. He promised to investigate a refusal to admit them to an FA coaching course but cautioned that the views of the FA Council had probably not changed. Sadly, he was right. But Taylor and her teammates did not go quietly. A petition was organised while Margaret Ashworth wrote to Prime Minister Harold Macmillan. He declined to intervene. The FA's ban would remain until the following decade.

41. Sheffield Wednesday seat cushion, 1960s

'Only 48 hours after the latest, strongest F.A. edict on tough play and tough fans, this is what eye witnesses report from Hillsborough: Aston Villa winger Jimmy MacEwan fell, bleeding, to the ground. [Bronco] Layne was ordered off by referee Wilson as the crowd booed and hurled scores of cushions on the pitch. Police halted a spectator who tried to dash on the field. Wilson turned to talk to other players and, as he did so, another spectator raced on the pitch, jumped on the referee's back and struck him.'

Daily Express, 12 November 1962

The cushions that rained down onto Sheffield Wednesday's pitch might seem quaint to modern eyes. However, at the time, they reflected an attempt to modernise the matchday experience of fans. That they were also used as improvised missiles, reflecting the ongoing challenge of fan behaviour as the association game approached its centenary.

These cushions could be hired for sixpence when sitting on the wooden seats in the main stand at Hillsborough and were used into the 1980s. By then the club was urging fans not to steal them as souvenirs 'If people want them, they can make us an offer.'[83] When they were introduced in 1961, it was in imitation of glamorous Real Madrid, where 100 attendants sold them on matchdays.[84] As crowd numbers declined in the 1950s, leading English clubs started to look to leading European clubs and sports like American Football for ideas to make the stadium experience more attractive. Hillsborough was at the forefront of these changes. Floodlights were added in 1957 and, in 1961, a brand-new North Stand costing £150,000 was opened. With 10,008 seats, it raised the stadium's seated capacity from 9,000 to 16,000. This was only the second cantilever stand in the country and the first to run the full length of the pitch. For Simon Inglis, a historian of sports architecture, the stand is 'like an architect's model of the dream stand of the future, a space-age stand'.[85]

It might seem amusing then that cushions like these were thrown from some of the best seats in the house. But for the football authorities, such disorder was unwelcome and England's top referee, Arthur Ellis, warned that wire fences, as used in mainland Europe, might soon be needed.[86] The use of cushions as missiles and the accompanying pitch invasion reflected a longer history of disorderly behaviour by fans, stretching back to the Victorian period. But by the end of the 1960s, a distinctive hooligan sub-culture had begun to develop, characterised by violence outside as well as inside the stadium.[87] Ellis' warning about fences came true and in 1977 they were added to the Leppings Lane and Kop ends at Hillsborough.[88]

'These cushions could be hired for sixpence when sitting on the wooden seats in the main stand at Hillsborough and were used into the 1980s.'

42. Official replica Jules Rimet World Cup trophy, *1966*

'You never really think these sort of dreams can come true. When you first go to Wembley to see the England team play, you think, I'd just love the chance to play on the pitch, let alone, you know, be part and parcel of the success like that.'

Bobby Moore [89]

On 30 July 1966, Bobby Moore led the England team up the Wembley stairs to the Royal Box, where Queen Elizabeth II handed the England captain the Jules Rimet trophy. England had just become world champions by beating West Germany 4–2 in the World Cup final. The 90,000-plus crowd at Wembley and millions watching on television witnessed Moore kiss and hold the trophy aloft, as he and the rest of the team paraded it around the stadium.

It was designed by French sculptor Abel Lafleur and made of gold-plated sterling silver, sat atop a blue base of lapis lazuli. The main body depicted the winged figure of Nike, the Greek goddess of victory, holding a cup.

The original trophy is now missing but that prestigious moment in England's history is powerfully represented in a replica made in secret by the Football Association in 1966. Four months before the tournament began, the original was famously stolen during a public exhibition at Westminster Central Hall. It was found a week later by Pickles the dog and his owner, David Corbett.

To ensure this didn't happen again, the FA asked jeweller George Bird to create a replica to use in exhibitions and official functions until the original was handed back to FIFA for the Mexico 1970 World Cup. FIFA had denied the FA permission to make a replica, so after 1970 it was hidden from the public and returned to its creator.

The original trophy was given to Brazil following their third World Cup win in 1970, as stipulated by FIFA President Jules Rimet, who in 1928 passed the vote to initiate the global tournament. The trophy was originally called 'Victory' but in 1946 it was renamed in honour of the man who helped bring the competition into being. In 1974 a subsequent trophy, known as the FIFA World Cup, was introduced and has been used ever since.

Thirteen years later, the original was stolen for the second time whilst on display in the Brazilian Football Confederation's building in 1983. Over the years there has been much speculation around its fate, but it has never been recovered.

The FA's replica had been kept under Bird's bed until his death, and it was eventually bought at auction by FIFA in 1997. Due to the high auction price, there was speculation the replica could be the original trophy itself, but FIFA's testing confirmed it to be the copy.

England's triumph in 1966 will always be immortalised in history with the trophy lost to it. 'My life has never been the same since,' reflected Sir Bobby Charlton, a key figure in that success on home soil, decades later. 'There isn't a day ever, goes past that nobody mentions the World Cup to me and '66. Even little lads now come to me. You know, what was it like winning the World Cup Bobby?'. [90]

43. Sir Geoff Hurst's World Cup final shirt, *1966*

'Many teams could probably have crumbled. The momentum was with Germany but because of the strength of the team and the strength of the character of the team, very quickly we brushed it off.'

Sir Geoff Hurst [91]

Sir Geoff Hurst is one of the most iconic England players in football history. On 30 July 1966, the West Ham striker's hat-trick propelled England to football immortality as they beat West Germany 4–2 in the World Cup final. A young man from Ashton-under-Lyne took centre stage, as the country became world champions.

It's ironic that England men's crowning moment on home soil was achieved wearing their red away kit, and broadcast on screens in black and white. Hurst's shirt from that famous day perfectly represents his legacy and was made by the Manchester-based kit manufacturer Umbro.

Hurst came into the team during the latter stages of the tournament, following an injury to Jimmy Greaves. He repaid manager Alf Ramsey by scoring the only goal in a 1–0 quarter-final win against Argentina and setting up Bobby Charlton's second goal in the 2–1 semi-final win against Portugal.

Many consider his three goals in the final as a perfect hat-trick, as each goal was scored with a different body part. England were down 1–0 after 12 minutes, courtesy of a Helmut Haller strike. Six minutes later, Hurst got his first via a free-kick by West Ham teammate Bobby Moore, as he equalised with a glancing header.

His second goal is one of the most contentious and defining moments in football history. Martin Peters had put England ahead on 78 minutes, only for West Germany's Wolfgang Weber to make it 2–2 and force the match into extra time. On 101 minutes Hurst

'His second goal is one of the most contentious and defining moments in football history.'

controlled a low cross from Alan Ball and shot powerfully with this right foot. The ball hit the underside of the crossbar and bounced downwards. The question was whether the ball had crossed the line.

Referee Gottfried Dienst consulted his linesman, Tofiq Bahramov, and the goal was awarded — but the debate has continued and some contemporary studies into the film footage have suggested the whole of the ball did not cross the line. 'I agree nothing's ever proved conclusively, that the ball was over the line,' conceded Hurst. 'But … the power of my belief, has always believed it was in.' [92]

Hurst completed his hat-trick in the dying minutes via another ball by Bobby Moore, who hit a long pass into his stride. The striker carried the ball forward and hit another powerful shot with his left foot as it flew into the net. The goal will forever be remembered alongside BBC commentator Kenneth Wolstenholme's words: 'And here comes Hurst. He's got … some people are on the pitch, they think it's all over. It is now! It's four!.'

'My father, who was an ex-pro with Oldham and Rochdale, spent hours and hours in my back garden in Chelmsford teaching me to kick with my left foot,' recalled Hurst. 'I owe a great deal to my father, God rest him.' [93]

> 'The goal will forever be remembered alongside BBC commentator Kenneth Wolstenholme's words: "And here comes Hurst. He's got … some people are on the pitch, they think it's all over. It is now! It's four!."'

'The ball was initially taken by West German forward Helmut Haller, who later claimed it was German tradition for the first goal scorer to keep the ball.'

World Cup final ball, *1966*

44.

This orange-coloured leather ball is one of the most iconic and popular objects in the National Football Museum collection: it was the match ball in the 1966 World Cup final. It is the symbol of the first and only time that England have won the tournament. In modern football, the match ball is replaced almost every time it goes out of play, but previously only one match ball would be used. There were a couple of spares in case the ball got damaged or broke, but in the game in 1966 this did not happen, so this ball was used throughout the entire final. So this really is the actual ball that ended up at the back of the net six times in the game.

British sports equipment brand Slazenger was tasked with making the match balls for the 1966 World Cup. The Challenge 4-Star ball that was selected was made of 25 rectangular leather panels and in three different colours: white, yellow and orange, with the orange one being selected for the final match.

And what a great final game it was to watch! England had hosted the tournament and reaching the final against West Germany at Wembley was the icing on the cake. Almost 97,000 spectators as well as more than 30 million television viewers around the country, watched Bobby Moore lead the Three Lions to glory with a 4–2 victory in extra time

The ball was initially taken by West German forward Helmut Haller, who later claimed it was German tradition for the first goal scorer to keep the ball. Footage of the teams meeting the Queen and receiving their medals clearly shows Haller with the ball under his arm. The ball was signed by both squads at the celebratory dinner after the game, and Haller then took it to Germany, where it stayed for three decades. Ahead of Euro 96, several newspapers ran campaigns to return the ball to England, where the tournament was being hosted, and eventually it was bought by the Mirror Group in partnership with Virgin and Eurostar. By that point all signatures on the ball had faded and rubbed off. However, the ball today bears one clear mark: 'U.G'. When the ball returned to England, illusionist Uri Geller signed it. He said it was his bid to 'energise' it and help the host nation to success at Euro 96 (they lost in the semi-final).

While being part of the National Football Museum collection, the ball has travelled extensively, especially during the game's 50th anniversary celebrations in 2016. It has been to numerous events and exhibitions throughout the UK, the Houses of Parliament and No 11 Downing Street, and has travelled internationally to countries such as Germany and Austria and as far as Japan. Nowadays the ball is very fragile, with its bladder perished and rattling inside the ball, the leather deteriorating and the colour fading, so it only leaves the museum on very rare occasions. And we also want to ensure the vast majority of our visitors can see the ball on their visit to our galleries and are inspired by its incredible story.

45. Knitted World Cup Willie, *1966*

Mascots have become a staple of large sporting events, particularly the FIFA World Cup, where they symbolise the host country's culture and spirit, often taking the form of animals or the local fauna. The trend of incorporating mascots into World Cup culture began in 1966 with the creation of World Cup Willie, a lion that became an iconic symbol of the tournament, who fans still fondly remember today.

World Cup Willie was created by freelance artist Reg Hoye, who had previously worked on illustrations for various publications, including Enid Blyton's famous children's books. Hoye was commissioned by the Football Association to design a mascot for the 1966 World Cup, which was being hosted by England. He came up with four designs — a boy and three different lions. One of the lions, inspired by his own son Leo, became the official mascot of the tournament. This lion was portrayed as a cartoon character with a 1960s mop-top hairstyle, dressed in a Union Jack shirt. The nickname 'Willie' derived from the FA's Chief Administrative Officer at the time, E. K. Willson, who apparently bore a remarkable resemblance to the designed mascot. World Cup Willie was born!

The debut of World Cup Willie sparked a wave of merchandise associated with the tournament. More than 70 different products featuring the lion's image were created and sold to fans during the 1966 World Cup. These products ranged from everyday objects like toys, money boxes and beer glasses to commemorative coins and even women's stockings! This marked a pivotal moment in the commercialisation of sport and large sporting events. The idea of mass-produced merchandise would go on to become a multi-billion-dollar industry, with each World Cup now seeing the release of a wide selection of branded goods available to buy. World Cup Willie is such an iconic mascot that even today a search on Ebay reveals more than 100 items still available to buy for avid collectors and enthusiasts.

This World Cup Willie was crafted using the official knitting pattern no. 9653, produced by Patons Publications in 1966. The pattern helped bring the mascot to life in a new way and allowed fans to create their own version of the beloved lion. It was kindly knitted for the National Football Museum by the donor of the knitting pattern in 2016 and has been part of the museum collection, which boasts a large number of mascots from international tournaments, ever since.

Ultimately, the introduction of World Cup Willie was a game-changer for the widespread use of mascots in future tournaments, and the commercial opportunities that came with them. Today, the tradition of World Cup mascots continues, with each host nation unveiling a new, unique character that represents their country and its culture.

46. George Best's Ballon D'Or, *1968*

'The idol of Manchester United soccer fans, George Best, who was elected 1968 "Footballer of the Year" last June, has now been chosen as "European Footballer of the Year" — the first player ever to receive these honours in the same year. With George Best's Soccer Annual (16s.) rapidly approaching 50,000 sales, and George Best's Soccer Annual No. 2 scheduled for publication this summer, Pelham cannot resist pointing out that this is their Best new year yet.'

The Bookseller, 11 January 1969

There was no bigger star in European football than George Best in the late Sixties. The Manchester United winger had been voted the Football Writers' Footballer of the Year for the 1967–68 season, when he had helped United win the European Cup, and was also the First Division's leading scorer that year. He then followed up those achievements by being awarded the Ballon D'Or, the European footballer of the year award, in December 1968.

Best was a supremely talented footballer, whose name was used to sell a variety of products, including books. His every move seemed to be reported on by this stage of his life.

> **'Born in Belfast on 22 May 1946, Best's football talent was spotted by United scout Bob Bishop. According to legend, he sent Matt Busby a telegram saying: "I think I've found you a genius."'**

Born in Belfast on 22 May 1946, Best's football talent was spotted by United scout Bob Bishop. According to legend, he sent Matt Busby a telegram saying: 'I think I've found you a genius.'[94] Best was 15 at the time and joined United as an apprentice, making his first-team debut at the age of 17 in 1963. By the end of the 1963–64 season, he had made 26 appearances and had also captained the youth team to FA Youth Cup success.

Best went on to play a major part in helping United to League success in 1965 and 1967, in addition to the 1968 European Cup.

Best's talent, looks and charisma made him a footballing superstar at a time when the game was getting more television coverage than ever before. He epitomised the glamour

> 'One of the greatest footballers of all time, this Ballon D'Or remembers a time when George Best's talents thrilled thousands at games across Europe.'

of the game as the 1960s moved into the 1970s. With his friend and Manchester football rival Mike Summerbee, he opened a fashion boutique in the city centre, adding to his status as a cultural icon. Unfortunately, his every move seemed to be reported on and his lifestyle off the pitch frequently hit the headlines. Alcoholism and related issues affected his health and in November 2005 he died of a lung infection and multiple organ failure. He was 59.

One of the greatest footballers of all time, this Ballon D'Or remembers a time when his talents thrilled thousands at games across Europe.

The Ballon D'Or had been established in 1956 by the magazine *France Football*, with Stanley Matthews winning the inaugural award. It was conceived by sports writers Gabriel Hanot and Jacques Ferran, and only European footballers were eligible to be considered until 1995, when it was expanded to include players of any nationality playing at European clubs. In 2007 it became a global prize with all professional players from around the world eligible.

Alfredo Di Stefano became the first player to win it twice (1957 and 1959) and Johan Cruyff was the first to win it on three occasions (1971, 1973 and 1974). Lionel Messi raised the bar with a fourth Ballon D'Or in 2012, and went on to receive the honour another four times.

Subbuteo, *1970s*

47.

'I could hardly wait to get home from school to lay out my pitch on the carpet of the front room and away we went. Spurs against Arsenal, Manchester United vs Wolves, the greatest teams in the land were at my fingertips. I had a League competition, a Cup, a League Cup, all of them fiercely contested, and all of them against myself.'

Terry Wogan

Growing up in the Republic of Ireland in the 1950s, the future TV presenter Terry Wogan became a devotee of a game sweeping across the British Isles: Subbuteo. What started as a cottage industry game became a factory-produced product that became popular around the world. The version you see here represents the game in its heyday in the 1960s and 70s. Alongside the key components of player and pitch are some of the large numbers of accessories that were sold, ranging from substitutes to TV camera crews. Look closely and you might spot Queen Elizabeth II with the FA Cup. In Wogan's days, the game was altogether simpler, with cellophane figures and no pitch players were advised to cut

up old black-out curtains instead. But what Wogan and so many other players over the years brought was their own imagination, placing themselves at the centre of the adult football world.

The game was invented by Peter Adolph in 1946.[95] He worked in the Pensions Office and spent his spare time collecting birds' eggs. But after observing the growing popularity of children's toys, he took out an advert in the *Boys' Own Paper*, despite having no product and having only just patented his game. He then went out of the country on business, only for his mother to telegram him to inform him that he had received £7,500 in postal orders, following 20,000 responses to his advert for a game that did not yet exist. He banked the money and then spent the next six months fulfilling orders. Over time the business expanded, with a wide range of additional products added to the football range and similar versions for cricket and rugby. In 1968, demand was outstripping supply, but no bank would invest. Instead, Adolph was bought out by the major games' producer Waddington & Sons for £232,000.

Subbuteo's success did not exist in a vacuum and in many ways its popularity reflected that of an existing tabletop game, *Newfooty*. It was created in Liverpool in the 1920s by William Keeling, whose nephews played a tiddlywinks-based game called *Shoot!* This relied on unappealing counters, and Keeling hit upon the novel feature of putting

'The game was invented by Peter Adolph in 1946. He worked in the Pensions Office and spent his spare time collecting birds' eggs.'

cardboard figures on small lead bases to be flicked around the pitch. It proved popular in Liverpool and league and cup competitions were set up. Like Peter Adolph, Keeling ran a small cottage-scale business but, fatally, did not patent his idea. Trying to upscale his company in the 1950s, it crashed after Granada TV moved an expensive TV advert to the wrong timeslot. Unable to move stock and pay a large tax bill, the business was wound up. Legend has it that Adolph bought up the company and burnt the remaining *Newfooty* games.

Oh, and in case you are wondering, the game's name is that of Adolph's favourite bird, the hobby, or Falco Subbuteo.

48. Gill Sayell's Copa 71 Women's World Cup kitbag, *1971*

'It was while I was playing for Thame LFC I was picked to play for Harry Batt in an unofficial England team. I was 14 years old! I played in the Women's World Cup in Mexico City 1971. The things I remember most of Mexico 71 were the crowds, the hospitality, the Azteca Stadium and the excitement of this massive occasion. We had television appearances, a cocktail party at the British Embassy and so many more events. I was in awe of it all.'

Gill Sayell [96]

In 2019, the National Football Museum hosted a reunion of women football players. Among the 50 attendees were members of Harry Batt's England team which represented the country at the Women's World Cup in Mexico in 1971. As well as sharing her memories of attending a major world tournament as a teenager, Gill Sayell kindly loaned this kitbag for display.[97]

It was provided by the tournament sponsors, the Italian drinks company Martini & Rossi. In 1970 and 1971 they supported two Women's World Cups organised by the International Federation of Feminine Football (IFFF). This interest was borne out of an earlier European tournament, the Coppa Europa Per Nazioni, also hosted in Italy in 1969 and where Batt had led England to third place.

As Professor Jean Williams explains in *A History of Women's Football*, Batt was a bus driver who formed Chiltern Valley in 1968–69 because his wife June had started playing football.[98] A member of the Women's Football Association (WFA), he was well connected to developments in the European scene. However, the WFA did not officially approve any of the England teams that Batt put together due to fears over losing government funding.

Undeterred, Batt selected his 1971 squad from Chiltern Valley and Southampton players. June acted as a chaperone, and another female pioneer, Pat Dunn, acted as a trainer. After she passed a referee's examination in 1969 the FA introduced a ban to stop women refereeing men's games. Together with the squad of 15 players and the Batt's son Keith as their mascot, they embarked on the adventure of a lifetime.

The opening games were played in front of 80,000 spectators, while the final between Denmark and Mexico attracted 110,000 fans, still a record crowd for any women's sporting event. Batt's side lost their three group matches but were hugely popular with Mexican supporters. For England player Leah Caleb, then only 13 years old, 'the Mexico trip was life changing, an experience beyond comprehension.'[99]

Sadly, the English press showed little interest in the competition. Furthermore, Batt and his wife June were banned for life on their return by the WFA for playing without permission, while the players received three-month bans. But the 2019 reunion helped bring their story into the limelight. In 2023, the documentary *Copa 71* brought it to an international audience, telling the story of the tournament as a whole and celebrating all the competing players.

Sue Lopez's WFA Mitre Challenge Trophy winners' cup, *1971*

49.

'Cup final day was fantastic. For me, it felt like being at Wembley. The feeling of lifting that cup is something that I will never forget, thinking that we had actually won it, and the feeling that after all that time the FA had finally recognised that women could play football.'

Southampton captain Lesley Lloyd [100]

The first women's FA Cup final took place on 9 May 1971 at the Crystal Palace National Sports Centre. It was then called the WFA Mitre Challenge Trophy, due to the sponsorship deal with the Huddersfield-based sports equipment company. Instead of medals, the winners received miniature versions of the trophy, like this one awarded to forward Sue Lopez. She was part of the Southampton team that beat Stewarton & Thistle 4–1. It is the first of seven cup final wins for Lopez as Southampton dominated the early history of the tournament, with the club winning eight finals and losing another two between 1971 and 1981.

The road to the first women's FA Cup started in 1969. In that year, the Women's Football Association (WFA) was formed, and the FA started the process of formally rescinding their 1921 ban, a process that would take two years. The first tournament attracted 71 entrants, including teams from Wales and Scotland (where the finalists Stewarton & Thistle hailed from), whose FAs still did not recognise women's football. Southampton's win was not without controversy. Southampton were viewed by many as being a Southampton League XI, rather than a club side, and would be later found guilty of misrepresentation by the WFA. They were fined £25 but allowed to keep the trophy.

The prize seen here forms part of a larger collection of more than 1,000 objects that the museum has received from Lopez. Since the museum opened, she has been an important supporter of its work, sharing objects and stories from her career. Hers is an important story, that started after being inspired by England 1966 World Cup win. From early games on Southampton Common in the era of the ban, she went on to play for Southampton, Roma in Italy, and unofficial and official England teams, winning a total of 22 caps for the latter.[101]

Her post-playing career is no less important, taking in coaching for the Hampshire FA, managing the Southampton FC's women's side, the Welsh international team, and posts with the WFA and FA. In 1999 she was named the *Sunday Times* Female Coach of the Year and the following year she was awarded the MBE for services to Women's Football. She has also written an important contribution to the history of women's football with *Women on the Ball* (1997), still an important work all these years later.

Jack Charlton's FA Cup final Leeds United tracksuit jacket, *1972*

50.

'Now it would be a great joy to me. When people in another five to 10 years or 20 years, discuss the great Leeds United team, when they talk about ... Bremner, Charlton, Hunter. Now that would really be a kick.'

Jack Charlton [102]

Nicknamed 'Big Jack', Jack Charlton is an Elland Road legend, having spent his entire playing career at Leeds United. His 20-plus years with the club started in 1950, when he was 15 years old, as, in common with other young players not offered apprenticeships he joined the ground staff following a successful trial. He had been recommended by his uncle, Jim Milburn, who played at left-back and Charlton initially played in the youth team. He made his debut on 25 April 1953 against Doncaster Rovers in a 1–1 home draw.

Charlton went on to make a club-record 773 appearances for the team and is also their ninth all-time top scorer with 96 goals. During Leeds United's most successful period under manager Don Revie, Jack helped them win the Second Division title in 1964, the League Cup in 1968, the First Division title in 1969, the Inter-Cities Fairs Cup in both 1968 and 1971 and the FA Cup in 1972.

Charlton's Leeds United legacy and the club's golden era is suitably represented in his FA Cup final tracksuit jacket from 6 May 1972. Charlton and his defence held firm as Leeds beat the cup holders Arsenal 1–0. On 53 minutes, Mick Jones cut back a cross into the penalty area and Allan Clarke powerfully headed past the Arsenal keeper Geoff Barnett.

'When we were kids, and we used to go to the park and play, I would go home for dinner, and he'd stay on all day. He loved his football ... Bobby Charlton is the greatest player I've ever seen.'

This was Charlton's final trophy win, and it fittingly completed his career haul of winning each top-flight domestic honour. The tracksuit jacket also captures Don Revie's influence, as in 1961 he changed the colour of United's kit from blue and gold to the white of Real Madrid, with the aim of emulating the Spanish club's success. The colour, and having Charlton's name on the tracksuit, were just some of many ways that Revie sought to modernise and boost the Yorkshire club's image.

After retiring from playing in 1973, Charlton became a manager and led Middlesbrough to the Second Division title in 1974 and Sheffield Wednesday to promotion from the third tier in 1980. He was appointed the Republic of Ireland manager in 1986 and took the country to their first European Championship in 1988, to the quarter-finals of their first World Cup in 1990, and to the last 16 at USA 94.

Along with all their other achievements, Jack Charlton and his footballing legend brother, Bobby, will forever be immortalised as part of the 1966 World Cup winning team. During their football careers, there was a healthy rivalry between the brothers, but it has been documented that they had a strained relationship at times. Despite this, one of the most moving moments between them was Jack's heartfelt speech as he presented Bobby with his BBC Sports Personality of the Year Lifetime Achievement Award in 2008.

'When we were kids, and we used to go to the park and play, I would go home for dinner, and he'd stay on all day. He loved his football … Bobby Charlton is the greatest player I've ever seen.' [103]

51. Liz Deighan's England cap, *1974*

'At one training session Vera [Eland] asked me if she could put my name forward for England trials, which were coming up in June 1974 at Birmingham. I had no idea how many teams were out there in the bigger football world and that there was an England team! At the trials I was in my element, all these good footballers together, all showing their skills, desire and passion to play for their county. I knew then I wanted more. The whole selection process took a few months to be completed. Then my day came, the letter I was yearning to have, I had been selected for the squad for the next England match against France in November 1974. I was ecstatic. All my prayers had been answered. I knew at that point my life would change forever, and it did!'

Liz Deighan [104]

While a variety of club sides – including Dick, Kerr Ladies, Manchester Corinthians and Chiltern Valley Ladies – had played as unofficial England teams in various tours and competitions, the first official England women's international team came following the establishment of the Women's FA (WFA).

Those involved in its establishment had to push for the lifting of the FA's ban, while also seeking to establish competitions and a representative team. The international committee of the WFA was chaired by Gladys Aikin from the Manchester Corinthians, with the first England women's manager being former Watford player Eric Worthington, who led his team to a 3–2 victory over Scotland in their first official fixture

The international cap shown here belongs to Liz Deighan, who was selected for her first England squad against France in November 1974. That game ended in a 2–0 England victory at Wimbledon's Plough Lane, with Deighan coming on as substitute. She went on to make 49 international appearances, scoring in the semi-final of the 1984 Women's Euros, as England progressed to the final (losing to Sweden on penalties). Domestically, she was a member of the St Helens team that won the Women's FA Cup in 1980.[105]

After playing her final international in 1985, Deighan coached the North West regional team in 1986–87, before being appointed the England Under-21 coach. In 1990, the senior team's manager, Martin Reagan, was unable to travel with the squad to a tournament in Bulgaria, and Deighan was asked to take his place for the competition. In 1989 she was one of the founders of Newton Ladies, which was renamed Knowsley Ladies before becoming the current Liverpool FC Women's team.[106]

Deighan's cap is unusual in that she wore it whenever she was selected to play for England, decorating it with badges from the places she visited while representing her country. These caps are especially significant because the WFA did not have a budget for them. Instead, they relied on Secretary Flo Bilton to make them by hand. Bilton based her design on a men's cap loaned to her by fellow Hull resident Raich Carter, a prominent footballer with Sunderland, Derby and Hull.[107]

52. Viv Anderson's European Cup medal, *1979*

'I don't think they can understand, unless you're in that skin, you can't really understand what's been said and why they're saying it.'

Viv Anderson [108]

Viv Anderson made history by becoming England men's first senior Black footballer on 29 November 1978. A pioneering figure in English football, he was 22 when he made his international debut in a friendly 1–0 win at Wembley against Czechoslovakia.

'I could hear the crescendo getting louder and louder as I walked out, it was just an unbelievable experience not just for being Black, but for playing for my country,' he recalled.[109]

Born in Clifton, Nottingham, Anderson was the son of Jamaican parents, and he endured overwhelming racial abuse as a player in the late 1970s. There were still not many Black players in England and that type of behaviour was commonplace on both the pitches and stands. He was a skilful, composed and consistent player, who had to deal with bananas and other projectiles being thrown at him every week. He went on to play for England for over a decade, gaining 30 caps and scoring two goals.

In overcoming that adversity, he helped to open the door for other Black players coming through. It is so important for young people's aspirations to be able to see people they identify with in footballing positions and in wider society.

His calibre as a defender and resilience as a person is fittingly represented in his European Cup winners' medal from 1979. On 30 May that year, he helped Nottingham Forest conquer Europe by beating Malmö FF 1–0 in the Munich final. The goal was scored by Trevor Francis, who nodded in a cross from fellow attacker John Robertson. Anderson was also an integral member of Brian Clough's Forest team which had won the First Division and League Cup double the year before.

Anderson's medal also represents a side who were dominant in Europe for two years running as he was part of the team that retained the continent's biggest prize in 1980. Along with Liverpool, Forest are the only other English side to successfully defend the European Cup.

Between 1974 and 1984, Anderson became a Forest legend, making 328 appearances and scoring 15 goals. He went on to play for Arsenal, Manchester United and Sheffield Wednesday. During the 1993–94 season, he became player-manager at Barnsley, before joining former Manchester United teammate Bryan Robson as assistant-manager at Middlesbrough. for seven years.

In recent times, the story of Plymouth Argyle player Jack Leslie has come to light. He was of Jamaican heritage and, in 1925, the first Black player to receive an England call-up. Tragically, he was later dropped from the squad and most likely denied the opportunity because of his heritage.

'History should be telling people these stories,' said Anderson. 'You know, they need to know. Here's me, got the first Black shirt. But there was somebody before me, who could have quite easily been it.' [110]

53. Photograph of Carol Thomas as England win the Mundialito, *1985*

'Lining up before the kick-off, listening to the national anthems and suddenly realising that this was the 50th time I had captained England (in my 55th international). In one year, 1985, I had become the first woman player to represent England 50 times and now I was the first woman player captaining them for the 50th time, and in a World Cup final … talk about the stars lining up for you.'

Carol Thomas [111]

This rare photograph from the collection of England international Angela Gallimore captures the moment Carol Thomas lifted the Mundialito (known as the 'little World Cup') trophy. Outside of the Pony Home International Championship in 1976, this was the first tournament success for the England women's team. England had narrowly lost the 1984 European Championship final. But this time they went one better, beating Italy 3–1 to lift the enormous trophy.

Little known today, the Mundialito tournament was a precursor to the FIFA Women's World Cup. Held five times between 1981 and 1988, it was an invitational tournament for leading countries. England won it twice, beating the hosts Italy on both occasions in 1985 and 1988.

Reflecting on that first triumph, Thomas explained that it was a hectic schedule, with the team flying out, playing a four-game tournament, and then returning, all within the space of seven days. England even faced Wales the day before they travelled to Italy, meaning that some players played five games in nine days. 'Can you imagine that in these days?' [112]

England started with a 1–0 defeat to Denmark. The next day, Kerry Davis scored in a 1–1 draw with Italy that kept England's hopes of reaching the final alive. After a few days of light training and tactical preparations, England played their first-ever game against the USA. While we now know the USA as one of the powerhouses of women's international football, in 1985 they were just beginning to emerge.

Gallimore scored as England won 3–1 to reach the final, although it came at some personal cost for her. 'I scored a diving header after a quick free kick,' she recalled. 'Jackie Slack (left-back) went down the wing and crossed the ball. I had managed to get into the box and dived to meet the ball.'

'I actually missed the final as I had broken my nose. I was hospitalised for two days but back to watch the final.' [113]

'Little known today, the Mundialito tournament was a precursor to the FIFA Women's World Cup. Held five times between 1981 and 1988, it was an invitational tournament for leading countries. England won it twice, beating the hosts Italy on both occasions in 1985 and 1988.'

This set up a final with the hosts Italy. It was watched by 10,000 spectators while the second half was broadcast on Italian television. The television coverage may account for why the game was held during the heat of the day, rather than in the cooler evenings, as had happened for earlier matches. Marianne Space (2) and Brenda Sempare scored the goals in a 3–2 win.

While it was televised in Italy, there was very little coverage of the tournament in England and few of the players families were able to attend. As Thomas explained, 'It is only later that the feeling of disappointment hits you when you realise that you were not able to share this moment of success in your life with family, friends and fans.'[114] This makes this photo even more important as a rare visual record of a memorable moment in the history of the England women's team.

As with the Women's FA Cup, the whereabouts of the Mundialito trophy are unknown. When the Women's Football Association merged with the Football Association in 1993, the WFA offices in Manchester were shut down. Some of their collection ended up at the FA headquarters in Soho and were then passed to the National Football Museum in 2001. But the trophy was sadly not among them. If ever found, the museum would love to display it so people can learn about this important moment in the story of the Lionesses.

54. Leeds Supporters Against Nazis pin-badge, *1988*

'The atmosphere at Elland Road was intolerable in 1987. Both the racism in the ground and the fascists peddling their filth outside.'

Member of Leeds Fans United Against Racism and Fascism (LFUAR) [115]

Before the inception of the Premier League in 1992, English football was in dire need of investment, development and rejuvenation. In the 1980s there were tragedies at Heysel, Valley Parade and Hillsborough stadiums, where people lost their lives. Margaret Thatcher's Tory government saw many of the game's issues as a social order problem and wanted to introduce identity cards in their 1989 Football Spectators' Act.

Hooliganism was increasingly associated with English football supporters as the wider country was becoming more socially and politically divided. The growing conflict between the government and the working-class trade unions particularly affected communities in northern industrial towns and cities like Leeds.

The social and political unrest in the West Yorkshire city was reflected in its football club. Leeds United were relegated to the Second Division in 1982, their fortunes a far cry from the glory era of manager Don Revie. The decay could be seen in the unashamed racist behaviour of some of the club's fans at matches and its 'firm', the Leeds Service Crew, had a reputation as one of the worst gangs in football hooliganism.

On matchdays the National Front (NF) would be outside Elland Road selling copies of their *Bulldog* magazine. 'I used to stand on the Lowfields terrace and people would be stood next to you reading the NF news and laughing at it. There were occasions where they actually had copies of *Mein Kampf* for sale,' recalled LFUAR co-founder Paul Thomas.[116]

However, Leeds has a rich history of activism, and it was part of the Rock Against Racism (RAR) movement that began in the mid-70s. In a reaction to racist attacks and growing support for the NF, the RAR community organised gigs and carnivals throughout the

'They went on to produce an anti-racist fanzine called *Marching Altogether*, which was intentionally designed to not tell fans what to think, but to encourage them to laugh at racists and not take part in those chants.'

country to bring communities together. Leeds held the final RAR carnival at Potternewton Park, Chapeltown, in 1981, with The Specials headlining.

To tackle the growing abusive behaviour the club was attracting, a group of fans formed the LFUAR in 1987, which broke new ground in this country. They started by giving out leaflets and badges, as well as a fixture calendar featuring a photo of two of the club's Black players alongside the Leeds captain. The DIY culture and heart on sleeve nature of this fan movement's actions is proudly represented in one of their badges from 1988.

They went on to produce an anti-racist fanzine called *Marching Altogether*, which was intentionally designed to not tell fans what to think, but to encourage them to laugh at racists and not take part in those chants.

Over time, the behaviour of fans at the ground changed, as well as the club's performance on the pitch. Howard Wilkinson's appointment in 1988 led to their promotion as winners of the Second Division in 1990 before becoming champions of England in 1992.

Paul Thomas added: 'Attitudes towards racism in society were changing ... we're winning the league with Chris Fairclough, Rod Wallace and Chris Whyte, and the fans are behind them. You're thinking, "Yeah, this feels a very different place from four years ago."' [117]

55. Liverpool scarf, laid as a tribute at Anfield after the Hillsborough tragedy, *1989*

'The people of Liverpool stood by us from the very beginning. They believed in us. They knew we were telling the truth. And that makes me so proud to be a scouser. Liverpool people will fight for what's right, what's just, what's proper.'

Margaret Aspinall, Hillsborough justice campaigner [118]

The Hillsborough Stadium disaster occurred on 15 April 1989 during the FA Cup semi-final between Liverpool and Nottingham Forest. A total of 97 Liverpool supporters would lose their lives and hundreds more were injured due to crushing in two overcrowded sections with high fences and narrow gates. The disaster, at the home of Sheffield Wednesday, is largely attributed to mistakes made by the police.[119]

The tragedy shook the world, and this scarf was one of the many tributes that were placed at Liverpool's Anfield stadium in the spontaneous mourning that took place in the days and weeks immediately after the disaster.

Hillsborough was the worst stadium disaster to happen in British sporting history. In 1902, 25 fans died and more than 500 were injured at a Home International game between England and Scotland at Ibrox Stadium, when the rear of the wooden Tribune Stand collapsed. In 1971 a crush on a staircase at the same stadium in Glasgow led to 66 deaths and more than 200 injuries. Leading up to the disaster, almost 40 people had died on the same staircase at various matches, but no measures were taken to improve safety. The Burnden Park disaster in 1946 claimed the lives of 33 people when a crush occurred at an FA Cup game between Bolton Wanderers and Stoke City. In 1985, a blaze at Bradford City's Valley Parade Stadium left 56 dead and more than 250 injured when the wooden roof of the main stand caught fire. The stand had been officially condemned and was due to be replaced with a steel structure before the following season, but it was still open and full of fans for the game between Bradford City and Lincoln City.

The 1990 report from the inquiry into the Hillsborough disaster, overseen by Lord Justice Taylor, made several recommendations to improve the safety of stadiums. Fencing was removed and many clubs replaced the terracing at their grounds with all-seater stands. These included Manchester United's Stretford End and Arsenal's North Bank in 1992, with Liverpool's Spion Kop and Aston Villa's Holte End following a couple of years later. Some clubs, such as Bolton Wanderers, Sunderland, Southampton and Derby County, moved from their old grounds to new sites as it was easier to incorporate the changes into new, purpose-built all-seater stadiums. Others reduced the capacity in their grounds to make them safer for fans.

The Liverpool scarf was lent to the NFM by the Hillsborough Family Support Group, which supported bereaved families and campaigned for justice for their loved ones for more than 30 years. In 2016, an inquest jury delivered its verdict that the people who died in the disaster were unlawfully killed due to gross negligence manslaughter.[120] The group disbanded in 2021 because 'it is now time for families to move on' and 'we have gone as far as we could come'.[121] The scarf pictured pays tribute to the victims of this tragedy and tells a sad and powerful story of stadium safety and the legacy it left for English football.

Gurnam Singh's referee shirt, 1989

56.

'I am very proud to be the first Asian on the League list. But really, it does not make that much difference. If you do your job as a referee properly, it doesn't matter whether you are black, white, blue or green.'

Gurnam Singh [122]

This football shirt highlights when accountant Gurnam Singh became the first Asian referee in the Football League in 1989, breaking down an important barrier. The game was a Third Division fixture between Tranmere Rovers and Rotherham United played in September 1989 and, as Singh explained in articles of the period, he was proud of getting on to the League's list. His focus was on refereeing to the best of his ability, and he received praise for his control of games. Like most match officials, there were critics at times, of course, but Singh was frequently praised, with the *Independent* claiming that in 1994–95 he finished first in a merit order of 49 referees.

As a trailblazer, Singh broke down barriers, but he also received abuse and was the victim of discrimination. In May 1999 he was told he had been removed from the national register of referees, and this seemed totally unfair based on his record. Two years later, an employment tribunal found that the Football League, the National Review Board (which then oversaw the promotion and demotion of referees) and two officials had racially discriminated against Singh. Alan Seville, a former regional referees co-ordinator who was responsible for assessing officials, said that it became apparent to him at an early stage that the referee had been unfairly treated by those who determined promotion. The Independent reported: 'Mr Seville recalled a meeting in which Ken Ridden, the FA's director of refereeing, is alleged to have said: "We don't want people like him in the Premier League."' [123]

'As a trailblazer, Singh broke down barriers, but he also received abuse and was the victim of discrimination.'

'It was inevitable I would get discrimination from the terraces. I did not think it would come from the football authorities.'

David Burns, the Football League's chief executive, apologised to Singh, saying: 'I acknowledge this ruling and accept that there was a lack of objectivity by the Football League in appointing referees in the mid-1990s. I trust that this matter can now be settled between the relevant parties without further court hearings. Any form of discrimination within football cannot be tolerated and it is up to us at the League to take a lead in this matter. On behalf of the League, I would like to express our sincere regret and apologies to Gurnam Singh that it was necessary for him to bring this case to a tribunal to get the redress that he had sought through the official channels.' [124]

Demonstrating how football behaviour was perceived at the time, Singh had commented during the tribunal: 'It was inevitable I would get discrimination from the terraces. I did not think it would come from the football authorities.'

In the years that have followed, considerable effort has been made by football authorities and clubs to stamp out discrimination from the terraces as well as in all other areas of football, but sadly it continues. Gurnam Singh's shirt is an important reminder of a trailblazer whose experience should always be remembered.

57. Justin Fashanu *Gay Times* cover, 1991

'Let's be honest. There's so much hypocrisy. There's so many people who are not what they say they are. It's not a big deal, in as much as, people either employ me for what I can do on the soccer field or not. You know, there's a lot of people who get up to a lot of things and I don't think that should affect whether you can play or not.'

Justin Fashanu [125]

On Monday, 22 October 1990, Justin Fashanu became the first openly gay male professional footballer in the UK, as *The Sun* newspaper printed an interview with the headline '£1m Soccer Star: I am Gay. Justin Fashanu Confesses.'

Fashanu had a promising early career at Norwich City, which culminated in him becoming the first Black footballer to be sold for £1 million, as he joined Nottingham Forest in 1981.

Four years later, he sustained a career threatening knee injury while playing for Brighton & Hove Albion. After undergoing surgery in the United States, he began playing again but he had been unable to fully resurrect his career.

Set against the homophobic backdrop of Thatcher's introduction of Section 28 (which banned the 'promotion' of homosexuality in schools) and the AIDS crisis, there were rumours about Fashanu's sexuality. Fearing that he was going to be outed by a national newspaper, he took matters into his own hands.

In July 1991, Fashanu was interviewed by the *Gay Times* for their 'Justin Fashanu: Soccer's enigmatic gay star' cover story. He spoke about how he had not anticipated the backlash that followed and that his football career suffered as a result. Fashanu's importance and struggle after coming out is well represented in this magazine feature as, apart from a two-year stint with Torquay United, he darted between teams across the world before retiring in 1997.

In March 1998, Fashanu was accused of sexual assault by a 17-year-old, in the state of Maryland in the US, where homosexuality was illegal. He was questioned by police but not held in custody. They later went to arrest him at home, but Fashanu had fled back to England, fearing he would not get a fair trial.

On the 3 May 1998 he was found hanged in a lock-up in Shoreditch London at the age of 37. In his suicide note, he denied the charges, stating that the sex was consensual. The inquest into his death recorded a verdict of suicide.

His legacy as a talented footballer and trailblazer for the LGBTQ+ community lives on through the Justin Campaign, which conceived and launched the international initiative Football v Homophobia. Fashanu's niece, Amal Fashanu, also founded the Justin Fashanu

Foundation, which campaigns against homophobia in football.

For more than 30 years, Fashanu remained the only prominent player in UK professional men's football to be openly gay, until Blackpool's Jake Daniels came out in May 2022. 'I want people to know the real me,' he declared. 'And lying all the time isn't want I've wanted to do, and it has been a struggle. But now I just do feel like I'm ready to be myself. Be free and just be confident with it all.'[126]

58. Paul Gascoigne's Spitting Image puppet, 1990

'I was leaving the World Cup, we weren't in the final and I was leaving some fantastic supporters who were there.'

Paul Gascoigne [127]

One of the most emotional and iconic moments in English football history is the footage and images of Paul Gascoigne, nicknamed Gazza, crying at the 1990 World Cup. England lost a dramatic semi-final penalty shoot-out 4–3 to West Germany and the 23-year-old held his shirt to his face as the floodgates opened.

Earlier in the game, with the score delicately poised at 1–1, Gazza had already famously fought back the tears in extra time. On 99 minutes he was booked for a late challenge on Thomas Berthold. Having already received a yellow in the second round 1–0 win against Belgium, his eyes welled up, knowing that even if England had won, his tournament was over.

The pictures of his teammate Gary Lineker, gesturing to the England bench with concern for Gazza, are etched in many people's memory. For all his unbridled footballing talent, this is the moment many people across the nation began to cherish Gazza. He showed the world's biggest stage that football meant everything to him.

It's important to note that football was in a dire state during the 1980s. Attendances had declined, English clubs had been banned from playing in Europe, hooliganism and firms were on the rise and people lost their lives in tragic circumstances. Against that backdrop, Gazza and the 1990 England World Cup team's performance captured the public's imagination and arguably contributed to the growth and rehabilitation of football. Two years later, the top flight of English football was revitalised with the arrival of the Premier League.

Gazza's high-profile emotional outburst and jovial nature are fittingly captured in his Spitting Image puppet. It features a water system, for the puppet's tears mimic and exaggerate him crying.

Spitting Image was a British satirical television puppet show that originally ran from 1984 to 1996. It was created by Peter Fluck, Roger Law and Martin Lambie-Nairn and featured caricature puppets of famous politicians, sporting icons, actors, musicians, religious figures, other celebrities and the Royal Family.

Gazza was capped 57 times for England and scored 10 goals between 1988–1998. The most high-profile strike of them all captured him at his best as he scored a sublime goal against Scotland at the 1996 European Championship, lifting a ball over Colin Hendry with his left foot and then volleying past the Scottish keeper Andy Goram with his right.

After playing for Newcastle United, Tottenham Hotspur, Lazio, Rangers, Middlesbrough,

Everton and other clubs, he called time on his near 20-year career and retired in 2004.

He has spent years battling health issues and addictions, such as alcoholism, and has said he doesn't want to be remembered for those struggles. Instead, he'd like to be remembered as that younger man on the pitch, where he longs to be. 'I still haven't coped. I hardly try and watch games because I still wish I was playing.'[128]

59. Wembley Stadium seats, *1990*

This row of five stadium seats will look familiar to every football fan as chances are that they have sat on a similar one watching their team at some point!

These seats are from Wembley, England's national stadium. It was built in 1923 as part of the 'British Empire Exhibition' in North London, but in those days the stadium had rows of foldable wooden seats for fans as well as both teams to sit on. The plastic seats were installed in the early 1990s, not as spectator seats though, but as the front-row seats for the staff and substitutes' bench. Wooden seats remained in other parts of the original stadium, which was demolished in 2000

The plastic seats were used by many famous managers and players at Wembley, such as FA Cup and League Cup finals, international games and all of England's matches during Euro 96, as well as the final. The last FA Cup game the seats were used for was on 20 May 2000, when Chelsea claimed the trophy with a 1–0 win against Aston Villa. The very last game at the old Wembley was on 7 October that year, when 76.377 spectators saw England slip to a narrow defeat against Germany in a World Cup qualifier against England.

The first seating in football stadiums consisted mainly of wooden benches or seats, but gradually evolved to meet modern demands as well as respond to safety laws. Moulded plastic seats attached to the terraces are robust, easy to clean and, when folded, rainwater can simply run off the seat without accumulating into a puddle. The long-lasting, durable nature of plastic makes them the ideal choice for seats that resist harsh outdoor conditions.

These plastic substitutes' seats are, however, still a long way from the comfort of today's offerings. At the top level, coaches and substitutes now have spacious, high-backed leather chairs available to them, sometimes even heated. But nothing beats that familiar memory of watching your team on a foldable moulded plastic chair next to thousands of fellow supporters on matchday!

'The last FA Cup game the seats were used for was on 20 May 2000, when Chelsea claimed the trophy with a 1–0 win against Aston Villa.'

'Nothing beats that familiar memory of watching your team on a foldable moulded plastic chair next to

thousands of fellow supporters on matchday!'

60. Replica Premier League trophy, *1992*

'We saw the repackaging ... Everybody had this opportunity now, to be seen out there ... It was a really exciting time.'

Brian Deane [129]

Between 1977 and 1984, English football clubs dominated the European Cup with Liverpool, Nottingham Forest and Aston Villa winning seven titles in eight years between them. However, the Heysel Stadium disaster, when 39 Juventus fans died in a crush before the Italian club's European Cup final against Liverpool in May 1985, led to all English clubs being banned from European competitions for five years.

During this time hooliganism was commonplace, many grounds were in need of investment, and a large number of people had lost their lives in tragic events at Valley Parade and Hillsborough stadiums.

The tide began to shift at the start of the following decade as England reached the semi-finals of the 1990 World Cup, the European ban was lifted and the Taylor Report recommended all major stadiums become all-seater.

The English First Division clubs believed the establishment of a new league was necessary to bring more money into the game and help it develop. Some of the biggest clubs in the country met with London Weekend Television (LWT) and Football Association executives to gain support and plan a breakaway from the English Football League, founded in 1888.

'Adorned with an eye-catching golden crown, the success and grandeur of the Premier League is perfectly represented in this replica trophy.'

'On 15 August 1992, Brian Deane headed the ball past Peter Schmeichel at 3:05pm and made history, becoming the first player to score in the inaugural Premier League.'

On 17 July 1991 they signed a Founder Member Agreement that established the basic principles to set up the Premier League. It would have commercial independence away from both the Football League and the FA, and on 20 February 1992, each First Division club resigned from the Football League.

The Premier League was formally established on 27 May as a limited company and a television deal was agreed with broadcaster BSkyB. It is important to note this meant LWT lost out, after being involved in early developments.

On 15 August 1992, Brian Deane headed the ball past Peter Schmeichel at 3:05pm and made history, becoming the first player to score in the inaugural Premier League campaign. He scored both goals in Sheffield United's 2–1 win against Manchester United. 'No mean feat, you know, because Peter Schmeichel was probably the best goalkeeper in the world at the time.' [130]

Adorned with an eye-catching golden crown, the success and grandeur of the Premier League is perfectly represented in this replica trophy. Over the years, the league has seen Manchester United win the most titles, Alan Shearer score the most goals and Gareth Barry play the most games.

It has established itself as arguably the best league in world football. Attracting the very best foreign talents and transforming teams line ups with players from all over the globe. TV coverage of games has continued to grow, along with the attendance at games and with the advent of android phones, the way fans engage with the league is forever evolving.

'It's the best league in the world,' added Deane. 'It's the most covered. It's changed the face of football in this country.' [131]

FA Premier League press release, 1992

61.

'Starting August 16, the record television deal for British sport will feature 60 live matches – each Sunday afternoon and Monday evening of the Premier League programme – on BSkyB; "Match of the Day" will return to BBC on Saturday evenings with recorded highlights, along with a significant support programming including the Saturday lunch-time preview programme, "Football Focus."

'Premier League Chief Executive, Rick Parry, said: "This offer was the clear unequivocal recommendation of the Chairman, Sir John Quinton, and myself to the 22 Clubs, partly because it offered this staggering sum in the short terms but largely because it offered football as a partnership with the broadcasters – a way forward to the 21st Century.
It is a visionary deal – a progressive deal – which enables football to have a say in its own destiny instead of being reliant on selling its rights to broadcasters without obligation."'

FA Premier League press release, 20 May 1992

In the early 1990s the English league structure, which had grown over the previous century, was transformed with the formation of the breakaway Premier League. Initially comprised of the 22 clubs who would have made up the old First Division of the Football League, it was set up in time for the 1992–93 season.

Breaking away from the Football League was not universally popular and debates had rumbled on for several years. This press release was significant as it highlighted a groundbreaking new television deal for the new competition. The number of live televised games had gradually increased during previous seasons, but this brought significantly more television coverage than had been experienced before. It also provided a major increase in the income football's top league was to receive.

This original press release comes from the collection of public relations man John Watt and was donated to the National Football Museum by his widow. In the 1970s, John had played his part in establishing the Manager of the Month award with Bell's whisky, which marked a new development in commercial sponsorship for the game. John annotated this press release with background information and his own research into the 1992 television deal. He attended several significant meetings behind the scenes and his handwritten notes add to our knowledge of these discussions. Significantly, one of his meeting notes is a quote saying: 'We are conscious of the problems that fixture disruption will cause to

THE FOOTBALL ASSOCIATION
LIMITED
Founded 1863

Patron: HER MAJESTY THE QUEEN
President: H.R.H. THE DUKE OF KENT
Chairman: SIR BERT MILLICHIP

Chief Executive:
R. H. G. KELLY FCIS

Phone: 071-402 7151/071-262 4542
Telex: 261110
Facsimile: 071-402 0486

16 LANCASTER GATE, LONDON W2 3LW

Our Ref: *Your Ref:*

THE FA PREMIER LEAGUE PRESS RELEASE

BSKYB AND BBC WIN PREMIER LEAGUE CONTRACT IN A RECORD BID OF £304 MILLION

The FA Premier League - consisting of England's leading 22 football clubs - accepted an offer of £304 million over five years from the satellite channel BSkyB and BBC - a composite offer to cover domestic coverage, overseas sales and sponsorship.

Starting August 15, the record television deal for British sport will feature 60 live matches - each Sunday afternoon and Monday evening of the Premier League programme - on BSkyB; "Match of the Day" will return to BBC on Saturday evenings with recorded highlights, along with a significant support programming including the Saturday lunch-time preview programme, "Football Focus."

Premier League Chief Executive, Rick Parry, said: "This offer was the clear unequivocal recommendation of the Chairman, Sir John Quinton, and myself to the 22 Clubs, partly because it offered this staggering sum in the short term but largely because it offered football as a partnership with the broadcasters - a way forward to the 21st Century.

It is a visionary deal - a progressive deal - which enables football to have a say in its own destiny instead of being reliant on selling its rights to broadcasters without obligation."

Registered Office: 16 Lancaster Gate, London W2 3LW
Incorporated in London   Registration Number 77797

"It will be the first time football has had a voice in the way the sport is covered on television."

A joint board of independent experts will be established immediately to oversee scheduling and programming standards.

"The BSkyB philosophy will encompass a broader spread of Clubs - not just coverage of the big games but ensuring that every Club will have live matches." explained Parry.

"Obviously, money was of fundamental importance - each Club will be guaranteed £1.5 million per season with a sliding scale rewarding League positions (the champions will receive £818,000, with the bottom Club getting £37,000) and facility fees for live matches in the first year will bring each participating club approximately £78,000 - but, to me, the energy and the imagination which BSkyB are going to put into covering the Premier League is almost of equal value."

For further details please contact:

Rick Parry
Chief Executive
The FA Premier League
Tel: 071-262 4542

fans. Consequently, we make every effort to ensure that no one club's fans will have their Saturday programme disrupted too dramatically.'[132] By the 2020s that idea seemed to have fallen away as some clubs found themselves rarely playing at the traditional time of 3pm on a Saturday.

One interesting aspect in 1992 is that the press release linked the new deal to more historical football coverage of the game. Note how it talks of *Match of the Day* and *Football Focus*, playing to the traditions and popularity of televised football. Both programmes were considered critical elements of football's television coverage and by mentioning those, it seems as if the press release was hoping to satisfy all football viewers.

There was criticism that free-to-air live games were not included in the deal and a group of 42 MPs raised their concerns. There was also legal action taken by ITV over the negotiations which had resulted in BSkyB's bid being accepted. Some football managers also criticised the deal, including Manchester United's Alex Ferguson. He was quoted in the *Sports Argus* on 23 May 1992 as saying: 'It's the most ludicrous decision football has taken.' [133]

From a monetary point of view, the news that all clubs would be guaranteed £1.5 million per season, plus appearance and performance fees, was welcomed by clubs who had feared that only the leading teams would benefit. Of course, this deal and those that have followed were for Premier League television rights and not for the Football League.

The first TV deal for live league games had come in 1983, when the BBC and ITV joined forces to pay £5.2 million over two years to show five top-flight matches per season. As a demonstration of how television rights have grown, in 2023 the Premier League secured a four-year deal worth £6.7 billion with Sky and TNT. Beginning with the 2025–26 campaign, the agreement gave Sky 215 live matches each season, including 10 fixtures on the final day, while TNT would have 52 live games. Match of the Day would continue to show highlights.

'One interesting aspect in 1992 is that the press release linked the new deal to more historical football coverage of the game.'

Hackney Women's FC pennant, 1992

62.

'The England women's team have got out lesbians playing, and there's girls there wanting their shirts, and don't think nothing about it. That to me is progression, you know that, you can't go back on that.'

Joanie Evans, ex-Hackney Women player [134]

Hackney Women's FC were founded in 1986 and made history by becoming the first openly gay women's football team in London and wider Europe. Set against the political climate of the AIDS epidemic and wider homophobia, this was a brave, bold and radical step by the club and many of its players had to deal with discrimination and prejudice.

Two years after the grass-roots club was formed, Margaret Thatcher's Tory Government introduced Section 28, of the Local Government Act 1988. This legislation prohibited schools and local services from teaching about same-sex relationships. It was in this politically charged environment that Hackney's trailblazers even faced some opposition from within the female football community itself, who felt the club could interfere with the progression of women's football. The FA had only lifted the 50-year ban on women's football in 1971, a damaging period which the women's game is still recovering from.

Hackney Women responded to the adversity by coming together to write a constitution that set themselves out as a women-run and majority-lesbian club. This was breaking new ground back then and, up to this day, the club stands by these ethics and philosophy.

They were also the first team to instigate a fair play policy, to ensure that all women are encouraged to train and play competitive football regardless of their skills, age, ethnic origin and sexual orientation. '[They] had women on all levels,' said former player Joanie Evans. 'Some that never kicked a ball and my thing is that anybody can play football. You know, it doesn't matter, they might not be brilliant, but anybody can kick a ball.'

Hackney Women's legacy as pioneers for the LGBTIQ+ communities in football is perfectly[135] represented in a pennant from the 1992–93 season. The black and red pennant portrays an image of two women embracing each other around a football, representing the club's pride and authenticity to the opposition and wider football community.

Over the years, the inclusive club has grown, and it now incorporates more than 100 players in its first and reserve teams, as well as beginners' activities. The club provides a safe place for all women to be and express themselves on the pitch. Whilst offering the opportunity to meet other people and build meaningful friendships. Hackney Women may now be 40 years old but in the current period of immense growth in the women's game and increased footballing initiatives and campaigns for LGBTQ+ communities, the club is still very relevant today.

'If you mention Hackney Women's, people always know about it,' added Evans. 'Doesn't matter where they're from, they seem to know about the club, because we've also maintained that sort of like fighter instinct. And that's what it's really about, no matter, yes, we're from Hackney but we can do all of these things.' [136]

'Hackney Women responded to the adversity by coming together to write a constitution that set themselves out as a women-run and majority-lesbian club.'

Jürgen Klinsmann's shirt, *1994*

63.

'A thousand fans in front of the stand were waiting for the Spurs bus to pull up, you know. And each had all signs ... holding it up in the air, 5.6, 5.8, 5.9. I said what is this about? The lads were cracking up on the bus. "Jurgen, this is for you. It's you're welcome to the Premier League ... they judge your diving!"'

Jürgen Klinsmann [137]

When Tottenham Hotspur signed 1990 World Cup winner Jürgen Klinsmann from Monaco in July 1994, the Premier League was only two years old and there were not many overseas players in it. The fans and media were more focused on the new £2 million signing's reputation as a diver, rather than his goal-scoring pedigree.

On 20 August, Klinsmann made his debut in an away match against Sheffield Wednesday. He made an instant impact, heading in Darren Anderton's cross and scoring Spurs fourth goal in a 4–3 away win at Hillsborough. Straight after scoring, in answer to the critics, he famously celebrated his header with a simulated dive. He was followed by several of his teammates, as they all went to ground towards the corner flag.

Klinsmann has stated the suggestion to dive after scoring on his debut came from his new strike partner. 'Teddy Sheringham said, "I have an idea. You score the first goal today ... you [have] got to do a dive, you [have] all got to do a dive." And I said okay and that's what happened. I scored a goal and the whole team ran at me and we kind of all dove in front of the Sheffield Wednesday fans.' [138]

The dive celebration became an instant hit, and it is an iconic moment in early Premier League history. It sparked adults and kids mimicking the celebration across the leagues and in park kickabouts. This shirt highlights Klinsmann's endearing qualities as Tottenham Hotspur fans, and football supporters across the country in general quickly fell in love with his personality as well as his footballing talents.

Even though he sustained a head injury in the first game, he made his home debut in the next match against Everton. The now iconic dive celebration was repeated as Klinsmann scored an acrobatic bicycle kick in front of the Spurs fans at White Hart Lane. The German grabbed a second with a header before half-time and the game finished 2–1 to home team. He scored 20 goals in the Premier League that season and 29 overall.

After just one year in north London, Klinsmann left for Bayern Munich, winning the UEFA Cup in 1996 and then the Bundesliga in 1997. He then moved to Sampdoria but returned to Spurs on loan in December 1997. This would be his final season playing top-flight football and his nine goals helped the club avoid relegation. 'Both experiences [at Spurs] were very emotional because they were always connected with the fans,' he later said.[139]

64. Ian Wright's Arsenal FC shirt, *1994*

'When you got people talking about you in that way and they [are] speaking about you so glowingly, it's magnificent, it's unbelievable. You know what I mean, all I ever wanted was to play at this level.'

Ian Wright [140]

The son of Jamaican parents, Ian Wright was born in Woolwich, London, in 1963. The ex-England international is a very important figure in the history of both Crystal Palace and Arsenal, as well as wider Black football history in England. He is now one of the most popular media personalities in football, but his journey into the professional game came relatively late. After several unsuccessful trials as a teenager, he played for Sunday League club Ten-em-Bee until he was 21.

Things quickly changed in 1985 when he was signed by semi-professional Greenwich Borough. Only a few matches later, he was spotted by Crystal Palace. Wright impressed Eagles manager Steve Coppell during his two-week trial and he signed a professional contract that August.

Wright is one of the most high-profile footballers to speak out about the adversity and discrimination he faced as a Black player making his way in the game. 'When I first signed for Palace, I got abuse in the changing room. It was just an accepted thing to do … If you're not somebody who is gonna laugh and joke about with it then, you're seen as, oh watch him, he's got a little bit of a chip on his shoulder.' [141]

In his fourth season at Palace, Wright's formidable striking partnership with Mark Bright was integral to their promotion back to the First Division in 1989. Two years later, he became a then club-record signing, as he was bought by Arsenal for £2.5 million. He took no time in making an impact by scoring on his debut against Leicester City in the League Cup.

'Wright is one of the most high-profile footballers to speak out about the adversity and discrimination he faced as a Black player making his way in the game.'

His prolific goal-scoring talents are fittingly represented in one of the Arsenal shirts he wore during the 1994–95 season. He scored 30 goals in 47 appearances overall, which was the third season in a row that he had reached 30 or more goals for the club. The tally is perhaps even more impressive given the club dismissed their long-time manager, George Graham, in February 1995 over allegations of illegal payments.

Even as the club struggled for the reminder of the season, Wright still scored 18 goals in the Premier League, and he grabbed three goals in the League Cup. He was at his most

clinical in the UEFA Cup Winners' Cup, as he finished the tournament's top scorer with nine goals in as many games. He scored in each round apart from the final, which the defending champions lost 2–1 to Real Zaragoza.

Following several cup wins with Arsenal, Wright fittingly ended his time with the club by winning the Premier League in 1997–98. 'Coming in so late [into the professional game] and realising that the opportunity I had I had to take full advantage, in every training session, every game,' he reflected. '[I] didn't want to leave anything out there.' [142]

65. Fantasy Football League sofa, *1994*

'Some of those players that we worked with, you know they were footballers, they weren't actors. They really struggled with the lines and delivering gags, as they have every right to. You know, if me and David Baddiel had been put into a football team, we would have struggled.'

Frank Skinner [143]

Fantasy Football League was a successful television comedy show that capitalised on the early rejuvenation of football in 1990s England.

Integral to its creation was the rise in popularity of the Fantasy Football game, which has its origins in 1960s American football. The basic premise is for participants to curate a fictional team of real-life players, who score points from their performances on the pitch.

It was presented by the comedians David Baddiel and Frank Skinner, who had been part of the original Radio 5 show. During each episode the duo would make jokes and sketches connected to recent Premier League events. They had a sidekick known as 'Statto', who was the sports commentator and pundit Angus Loughran. He would be dressed in pyjamas and was the main source of facts and statistics.

The studio backdrop was made to look like a flat where the football-mad hosts lived. Celebrity guests would ring the doorbell and then take a seat on the sofa, as they talked through their fantasy football teams. The show's tone and imagery are fittingly represented in the sofa that Baddiel and Skinner sat on, as they talked to viewers as if they were at home themselves.

For all the show's success, it wasn't without its controversy as in a particular racist sketch, Baddiel offensively 'dressed up' as Jason Lee, wearing black make-up and a pineapple on his head. After many years, Baddiel met with Lee and apologised for the harm he had caused him, as the two discussed its ridicule of Lee's cultural identity and heritage. 'As soon as I saw the first sketch, you know, my heart dropped,' the ex-Nottingham Forest striker said. 'I'm not going to lie, I though wow ... seriously violating me in every single way possible.' [144]

The show, which was launched in 1994, ran for three series and was followed up by a special during UEFA Euro 96, at which time Baddiel and Skinner's *Three Lions* England song with the Lightning Seeds was number one. The show was revived by ITV for live specials during the 1998 World Cup and the 2004 European Championship. It was again recently revived by Sky between 2022 to 2024 with new hosts Elis James and Matt Lucas.

> 'Celebrity guests would ring the doorbell and then take a seat on the sofa.'

The show had several regular features but perhaps the most fondly remembered is 'Jeff Astle Sings'. Skinner's West Brom hero would comically sing a song as the episode ended and credits rolled up.

'He still liked the crowd, he loved that big cheer when he came on, and he loved being at the centre of it, you know, which is what he'd been like as a player.' [145]

66. Photograph by Chris Unger of England v Nigeria, *1995*

'One thing for sure, Chris had a great love of the game. I had no idea how big this collection of women's football became until Chris became sick. I learned that Chris was sending equipment and money to female players in poor places in the world. He would give everything he could. I found out to what level after he passed by receiving phone calls and emails from all over the world.'

Kenneth Unger Jnr, brother of Chris Unger [146]

This photograph captures England scoring in their first FIFA Women's World Cup. The tournament was held in Sweden in 1995 and, in their final Group B game, England played Nigeria before 1,843 fans at the Tingvalla stadium in Karlstad. The photograph is taken from just to the left of the Nigerian goal, providing a great view of Karen Farley's opener in the 10th minute. England proceeded to the knock-out stages with a 3–2 win but were eliminated by Germany in the quarter-finals.

This photograph was not taken by a professional photographer but by telephone repairman, women's football coach and memorabilia collector Chris Unger. It is one of nearly 200 photographs that Unger took at the World Cup in Sweden. Unger was not only a collector of women's football history, but he also helped record it at a time when it still attracted relatively little attention in many countries.

He covered at least six matches, including the final between Norway and Germany and the third-place game between China and the USA. Sadly, we currently know little about how Unger's role as a photographer worked, so we don't know whether he chose these games or whether they were allocated to him. But to our delight, we found that 127 images related to England's matches at the tournament, providing a rare visual insight of England on the world stage.

After their successes in the Mundialito tournaments of the 1980s, England failed to qualify for the first official FIFA Women's World Cup in 1991. Hosted by China, the trophy was won by the USA, where there was strong support for grass-roots girls' and woman's

'Chris was just a regular working man, he worked 44 years for the local phone company as an outside repair man.'

football. Unger was one of the many coaches involved at this level and his brother, Kenneth, explained that after playing, Chris had moved into coaching girls' teams in the 14–19 age range, going as far as to visit Europe with them. Like many grass-roots coaches, he did this purely in his own time as, 'Chris was just a regular working man, he worked 44 years for the local phone company as an outside repair man.' [147]

Chris Unger's passion for the women's game led him to Sweden, where he helped create a special visual record of the World Cup. The images of England are the largest collection the National Football Museum has for the national side at any tournament. These alone would make them very special but they are just a small segment of the many riches contained in a collection Unger spent more than 30 years creating.

67. Championship Manager, 1996-97

'You can read a book in a few days and be in that universe, but you can't affect anything. Whereas with Football Manager, every single thing you do affects everything in the universe.'

Miles Jacobson OBE, CEO of *Sports Interactive*, 2014 [148]

'Football admin, that's what it is, and you know it's strange, because I don't really enjoy doing my own admin, yet here I am, spending hours and hours of my life simulating the administrative duties of somebody else.'

Iain Macintosh, comedian and author of *Footballer Manager Stole My Life*, 2014 [149]

Brothers Paul and Oliver Collyer started making their first football computer games in 1985 – while still at school.[150] In 1992 they released *Championship Manager* and tried to interest publishers. Electronic Arts, one of the largest companies at the time, turned them down due to the lack of in-game graphics, but Domark took a chance on them. In 1994 the brothers founded *Sports Interactive* and were joined in 1997 by Miles Jacobson. With his help, the business has grown from a few individuals to more than 100 staff, supported by several thousand researchers. Together, they produce one of the most popular football games for personal computers, now known as *Football Manager*.

The copy of *Championship Manager 1996–97* you see here was the first seasonal update provided to *Championship Manager 2*. In the late 1990s and early 2000s the game's popularity skyrocketed, with 20 million copies sold by 2014. The level of detail increased with each edition, reflecting changes in real-life football, such as the Bosman ruling that increased players' freedom of movement. Such was its popularity that even professional players played the game. Over time it developed further crossovers into real life. In 2014, the game's publisher signed a deal to supply information to data analysts Prozone to help clubs scout players.

But the game's realism and attention to detail is only one part of its story. As with *Subbuteo*, players brought their own creativity and imagination to a game that, for many years, relied on simple text to narrate the course of a game's events (2D and 3D match engines were added in time). Wearing suits for cup finals, setting fire to paper in baskets to simulate the flares lit at European away games, making testimonial programmes for beloved players; these were just some of the ways that players immersed themselves. Such dedication could be costly though, with 35 divorce cases in one year citing the game.

Over time, footballers within the game, both real and fictional, have developed cult-status. To mention Tonton Zola Moukoko, Mark Kerr or Freddy Adu to players of a certain

age is to bring back fond memories of World Cup or Champions League winning sides formed around these star players, all of whom sadly never quite matched the futures predicted for them.[151] After Cherno Samba scored 1,000 goals for Alex Ireland's Millwall side, he bought a full kit with 'Samba 9' printed on the back. 'I still remember the awkward conversation with the club shop staff when making my order by telephone,' he recalled. 'It's still in regular use for five-a-side games.'[152]

68. Robbie Fowler's FA Cup final Armani suit, *1996*

'It probably wasn't the greatest thing to do but look if we'd have won it they would have been the best suits in the world.'

Robbie Fowler [153]

On 11 May 1996, Liverpool played fierce rivals Manchester United in the FA Cup final. The match did not live up to expectations as, after a bright start, the crops of young talented players on both sides failed to flourish.

The final is famously remembered for two reasons. The first is a famous moment on the pitch, when Eric Cantona won the game on 85 minutes. David James punched a corner ball into the penalty area and Cantona composed himself at the edge of it, striking the ball through a crowded box and into the net.

The second is vividly represented in Fowler's jacket, for a moment off the pitch, as Liverpool's players infamously walked into Wembley wearing unorthodox cream-coloured Emporio Armani suits. They were seen as quite outlandish and flamboyant. In stark contrast, the Manchester United players wore traditional navy suits. 'I was a young lad in the squad, it had nothing to do with me,' Fowler protested in 2022.[154]

Many of those young Liverpool stars had high-profile endorsements and were part of the increased commercialisation of Premier League footballers. They included some of the country's most exciting contemporary players in Jamie Redknapp, David James, Steve McManaman and Robbie Fowler.

When Gérard Houllier took charge in 1998, several of the group were sold but Fowler was kept on as a key part of the club's rebuilding. He played an important role in the Reds' 2001 treble success, winning the FA Cup, League Cup and UEFA Cup, and scoring in the latter two finals.

Of all the players who were sold under the Houllier rebuild, perhaps the most successful was Steve McManaman, who left in 1999 and went on to win two Champions Leagues and two La Ligas with Real Madrid.

Leading up to the 1996 FA Cup final, Fowler produced his best scoring return in his entire career. Forming a prolific goal-scoring partnership with Stan Collymore, he netted 36 goals in 53 appearances.

'If anyone is getting married and they want to borrow a cream suit, then you know, I'm your man.'

Over the years his ruthless ability to put the ball in the back of the net earned him legendary status at Liverpool. In his two spells for the club, he made 369 appearances and scored 183 goals. His 163 Premier League goals also make him the competition's ninth-highest scorer of all time.

When asked about the Armani suit again in the build-up to Liverpool's FA Cup final win over Chelsea in May 2022, Fowler joked, 'They're quite infamous the suits, aren't they? So, if anyone is getting married and they want to borrow a cream suit, then you know, I'm your man.' [155]

69. 'Looking Up Sunderland v Coventry City' by Stuart Roy Clarke, *1996*

'The thing that makes it stand out is the sense of wonder as they look out. I think the goalie had just tipped a shot over the bar, but it could just as well be a spaceship landing at Roker Park. The red and white is almost dripping off the shirts and there's a unique feeling about it … In many ways this photograph goes beyond football and maybe that is what appealed to Andrew Lloyd Webber.'

Sunderland Daily Echo [156]

Football photography can capture great goals and wonderful achievements, but images can often be more powerful when they show the crowd, or general football scenes. During the 1990s and 2000s, photographer Stuart Roy Clarke attended games looking for moments to capture. His images often show the culture of football in a way that regular matchday photographers did not at the time. The image shown here came from a Sunderland–Coventry game in 1996 and captures a fleeting moment when the anticipation of what could happen can be seen all over the faces of the Sunderland fans behind the fences at Roker Park.

This image is a wonderful example of Clarke's passion for making the ordinary special. No one in the photograph is posing, or seemingly aware of being photographed. They are engrossed in the game and Clarke has captured a moment all fans can recognise.

Over time the significance of this image, and the rest of Clarke's work, has increased. Sunderland left Roker Park in May 1997 having been given special dispensation to allow standing at the ground during the previous season. Terracing like this was disappearing (Fulham were allowed terracing for one season following their promotion in 2001), as was fencing at the front of stands. Another aspect captured here was the significant use of replica shirts – a decade earlier there would have been considerably fewer on display. By the mid-1990s the replica shirt industry had grown significantly, whereas earlier times had seen shirts worn infrequently, usually for special games like FA Cup finals or other Wembley trips.

The composer Andrew Lloyd-Webber saw the image in 2000 and was struck by the boy stood open-mouthed with both hands on the vertical fence bars. He wanted the boy's face to be the image and inspiration for a new show he was developing with Ben Elton called *The Beautiful Game*. An appeal to find the young supporter followed and Sunderland season ticket holder David Orr junior was eventually identified as the boy.[157] Orr's face was featured on posters and memorabilia connected with the musical, though some artistic licence was used – the shirt being worn was turned into a generic green shirt with a white round collar, rather than a Sunderland one!

'This image is a wonderful example of Clarke's passion for making the ordinary special.'

This photograph is part of Stuart Roy Clarke's *The Homes of Football* series. These images were taken on a Bronica camera with a standard lens and were not cropped, with his first photo in the series being of four boys at Clydebank's Kilbowie Park in 1989. Like Roker Park, this is another ground that has since been demolished. Other grounds, such as Maine Road, were also captured in their final days by Clarke.

Fly Me To The Moon, Middlesbrough fanzine, 1997

70.

'Middlesbrough's pre-international break victory over Leicester City was a reason for double celebration for many Boro supporters, particularly those with any kind of connection to the fanzine *Fly Me To The Moon*. Set up by Andi Gillandi, Robbie Boal and Tony Pierre, and named after Bruce Rioch's famous quote about Tony Mowbray, the first edition went on sale exactly 35 years ago this Sunday. That first edition saw 50 copies produced, but issue 640 which came out for the Leicester game had far more than that. Typifying the dedication of Boro fans, it remains one of the oldest football fanzines in the country still going, and now has more back issues than any remaining fanzine.'

Teesside Live [158]

There had been football fanzines in the 1970s, such as *Foul*, but it was during the 1980s that supporters at most clubs adopted the same punk DIY approach that had seen fan-produced music publications emerge. It was a decade when the game faced several challenges including hooliganism, club mismanagement and dilapidated grounds, with fans feeling their voices were not being heard. Often blamed for the ills in the game, supporters sought ways to ensure they were heard, and the fanzine movement was part of that.

Prior to the establishment of fanzines, supporters' opportunities to be heard were limited. Fans could call a local radio phone-in show, write to a local newspaper or to their club, but these were individual acts that rarely led anywhere. Then fanzines started appearing and supporters found a place where like-minded supporters gave their views on their club. Speaking in ways that resonated with fans, fanzines were not the corporate or conformist voices of the club.

From 1985 until the early 1990s, there was an explosion in the volume of unofficial club magazines produced and their establishment helped to bring a better understanding of what it was like to be a fan. Various initiatives were promoted and editors of fanzines from rival clubs often worked together, most notably campaigning against the introduction of ID cards, and in the aftermath of tragedies. Fanzines challenged the way the Government and authorities had characterised fans, while also providing a critical, unvarnished and humorous view of their own clubs. Sometimes they were light-hearted and at other times they questioned the directors of their own clubs.

The establishment of fanzines helped to change the way some clubs were run, while also helping to change perceptions of fans. Many fanzine writers went on to work in traditional media, demonstrating why supporter voices needed to be heard in the first place.

Middlesbrough's *Fly Me To The Moon*, launched in 1997, was one of many fanzines that emerged. 'The great thing is, we've always had the appetite from people wanting to write,' editor Rob Nichols explained in 2023. 'People would buy it, read it, and then they'd get in touch wanting to contribute. It was a new thing that you could write about your team. I'm finding now that some of the new writers are doing it because their parents are doing it. That doesn't make me feel old at all! Keeping that community spirit alive has been central, I think, to the success of it.' [159]

Technology has given supporters a variety of platforms, including online forums and social media, and these have led to the demise of many fanzines but some have found a new home online. Those that survive remain an important outlet for the voices of fans.

'The establishment of fanzines helped to change the way some clubs were run.'

Denis Irwin's shirt, *1999*   71.

'The one thing about us in 1999 is that we had great belief in ourselves.'

Denis Irwin [160]

Nicknamed 'Mr Dependable' for his efficiency, consistency and longevity, legendary fullback Denis Irwin is one of the most successful Irish footballers in history. During his 12 years at Manchester United, he won every major honour between 1990 and 2002. His trophy haul includes seven Premier Leagues, two FA Cups, a League Cup, a UEFA Cup Winners' Cup and Champions League title.

The most famous of those trophies came on 26 May 1999 as Manchester United made history by becoming the first English club to complete the 'Treble'. Winning the Premier League, FA Cup and UEFA Champions League in the same season.

In the final game of a long campaign, the Red Devils were trailing 1–0 to Bayern Munich as the game went into three minutes of injury time. It was Alex Ferguson's two second-half substitutes who would create the headlines. They were desperately pushing for an equaliser when Ryan Giggs's tame shot fell straight into the path of Teddy Sheringham, who steered the ball into the net. It appeared as though they would force the game into extra time but, seconds after the subsequent kick-off, they scored the winner.

David Beckham swung a corner in and Sheringham nodded the ball on and across the face of goal. In that moment, Ole Gunnar Solskjær reacted fastest as he poked the ball into the roof of the net, in front more than over 90,000 people at the Nou Camp Stadium. The 1998–99 season was filled with late comebacks for the team, but none were more dramatic than that final game.

Irwin's importance to the club's European success that year is well represented in his Champions League final winner's shirt, as he played in all but one of United's 13 games in their glorious run.

Born in Cork, he first played in England for Leeds United and Oldham Athletic in the Second Division, before moving to Manchester. He is regarded by Sir Alex Ferguson as one of his greatest signings.

During Sir Alex's 26-year tenure at Old Trafford, he is said to have built three great sides, which hit their peak in 1994, 1999 and 2008. Irwin played a key role in the first two of those great sides. Many established players made way in 1995 for the talented 'Class of 92', who were coming through the club's youth system. Irwin was one of the few to keep his place.

'The '94 side weren't as easy on the eye as the '99 team, and there weren't as many options, but we had guts and won the Double,' he later reflected. 'I loved playing with that team, and the XI was pretty set. Nothing can top '99 – we had drive in abundance, and goal scorers all over the pitch. I'm one of the few that played in both teams.' [161]

'The 1998-99 season was filled with late comebacks for the team, but none were more dramatic than that final game.'

'The tournament was a great success, and FIFA announced the establishment of the Women's World Cup, starting in 1991.'

Women's World Cup fan drum

72.

This is a 1999 FIFA Women's World Cup branded jingle drum, sold to fans attending the tournament in America. The drum features the official slogan for the World Cup – 'This is my game. This is my future. Watch me play' – and signifies the turning point for the women's game on many levels.

Women's football gained popularity following the lifting of restrictions on female access to football by many national governing bodies and competitions. There were unofficial World Cups in 1970 and 1971, in Italy and Mexico respectively. After that, the Mundialito (Spanish for 'little World Cup') was held five times, hosted by Japan in 1984 and then in four successive years by Italy. Italy won the competition three times and England twice. There was also the Women's World Invitational Tournament, organised by the Chinese Taipei Football Association, between 1978 and 1987. It was held four times in Taiwan. International competitions such as these put pressure on FIFA to organise its own competitions, and in 1988 the first FIFA-organised women's football tournament was held in China. Twelve teams from six confederations competed and Norway beat Sweden in the final in front of more than 30,000 spectators to lift the trophy. The tournament was a great success, and FIFA announced the establishment of the Women's World Cup, starting in 1991.

The inaugural competition was held in China and won by the USA. Sweden hosted the tournament four years later, with Norway lifting the trophy. But it was going to be the 1999 Women's World Cup that was going to change the landscape of the women's game forever with record attendances, viewership and global impact. Women's football at the 1996 Olympics in Atlanta had seen large crowds and expecting the World Cup to be similarly popular, all games were played at American football venues. Matches were attended by an average of 37,000 fans and the total attendance was more than one million. The final, played at the Rose Bowl in Pasadena, California, was attended by more than 90,000 spectators and saw the US national team beat China 5–4 on penalties.

The tournament was a turning point due to a number of factors – it benefited from American expertise in marketing and sponsorship, it pulled in large crowds and the host nation winning the tournament attracted huge media attention, which led to boosting the game in the USA and turned its leading players into megastars. This helped the whole of women's football to be taken seriously and showed the world what the female game could be. This small drum featuring the inspirational message of the tournament is a small reminder of where the women's game was before 1999 and where it is today.

73. *Daily Telegraph* Fantasy Football supplement, *1999-2000 season*

'I guess you'd call it an old-school start-up … I didn't have any money … I locked myself away for three months, designed the system and then started placing ads in football magazines … I remember printing out reports on a Sunday night and taking them down to the post office in big sacks. It feels very archaic now.'

Andrew Weinstein [162]

Today, online Fantasy Football is an extremely popular global game. The Premier League's official version has three and a half million players for the 2024–25 season. Using a set budget of £100 million, players compete to pick the most successful team from players across the league. Before each transfer deadline, players will pour over the latest stats and selection rumours before picking their team.

The documents you see here represent the game at the height of its pre-digital form in the UK. The concept is a US one, emerging first with American football in the 1960s and then baseball in the 1980s. Andrew Weinstein is credited with introducing and popularising the concept to Britain after seeing its popularity when visiting a family friend in the States.[163] He started by placing adverts in football magazines for information packs to help players run their own leagues. Players would then have in-person meetings to buy players and then any changes were submitted to Weinstein, with his fax machine going into overdrive on Fridays. He then watched the matches to work out the scores and posted the scores the following Tuesday.

Much like *Subbuteo* and *Championship Manager*, the business of fantasy football started out on a cottage scale. In the first season of 1991–92, Weinstein had about 600–700 players in 80 leagues. It was soon boosted by his appearances on a BBC 5 Live radio show called *Fantasy Football* alongside host Dominik Diamond and comedians David Baddiel and Frank Skinner. The latter two went onto host the TV version of *Fantasy Football*. In 1994, Weinstein worked with the *Daily Telegraph* to create the first mass-market version, with other newspaper imitating it after it proved a huge success. Out of a total circulation of 900,000, Weinstein estimated that, 350,000 of the *Telegraph's* readers signed up.[164]

The documents and rules from 1999 might elicit nostalgia from those who played at the time. Players filled out scores themselves and had to contact the newspaper to make transfers – these had to be made by post several days in advance, unless you rang an expensive phone line. Confirmation was sent via postcards like the one seen here. There was a maximum of 24 transfers per season, compared to weekly ones allowed in the modern game. All teams played a 4-3-3 system, compared to variations allowed in modern games, while the budget was £50 million.

The *Daily Telegraph* offered a cash prize of £25,000 for the overall winner in 1999 but most players play for more important stakes – bragging rights at work or among friends. Like *Championship Manager*, these included professional players and in the *Telegraph's* info pack, it names the most successful manager of the past season playing in the Premiership as one Gareth Southgate of Aston Villa.

TELEGRAPH PREM

The best fantasy-based football game in Britain – we are off

When it comes to fantasy-based football games, we at The Daily Telegraph try to remain one step ahead of the pack. And it's no different as we move into the new Millennium. In association with The Bank of Scotland, we've teamed up again with the best, most passionate and most exciting football league on earth, The FA Premier League, to bring you the ONLY officially endorsed fantasy-based football game. And this season, there are a few things you need to know about our game which makes the rest look like they are playing in the Dr Martens Southern Division:

Off, off, off...
There's no excuse to be slower than Southampton's back four and delaying the sending of your team. For the first time, we have supplied everything you need in this pack; your application form and the list of players with their scores from last season to help you out are here. The scoring system, prize info and details of how to play are all in this pack, too. It only takes a few minutes to pick a team and then you can start scrapping with the rest from August 7.

Out, out, out...
Thanks to the biggest change in football since long shorts became short and then long again, you can now make telephone transfers to your TPL team right up to the kick off of each match. So, on match days, you can check whether your goalkeeper has done a groin in the pre-match warm-up and if he has you can get shot of him with just one phone call. Any new players will score points immediately. This revolution in football games replaces the use of substitutes from last year. Note as well that for the first time we are not limiting the amount of players you can select from one Premiership team (the only selection restrictions are money and team formation), making transfers easier and quicker.

Take on your mates
Get a load of you to enter all your teams into one league - a Super League - and we'll supply you with up-to-date info on each of the teams in your Super League every fortnight. You'll still get to play in the main game, and your Super League will be taking on all the others across the country. It's the best way to play, you get more info and there are more chances of winning cash. And it's a bargain. To enter one team as an individual it costs £2 (two first-class stamps for under 18s) and now it can be as cheap to enter a Super League.

Our price structure for Super Leagues is as follows:

No of teams in your Super League:	Cost per manager
5-9	£5
10-14	£4
15-19	£3
20 or more	£2

EVERY Super League chairman will receive a FREE copy of Kick Off 'the official Premier League fans guide' worth £6.99.

EVERY PREMIER LEAGUE TEAM REVIE

Your full guide to the seas

OFFICIAL SPONSOR OF

in association with FourFourTwo

Free exclusiv

We've joined forces with the top footy m
This brilliant mag includes a club-by-club
sheet for this one. The magazine is only

10 interesting things you probably **didn't know** about last season:

1 The leading points scorer was **Jimmy Floyd Hasselbaink**
2 The player with the most key contributions was **David Beckham**

Much like Subbuteo and Championship Manager, the

Teamtalk...

1 **You're the gaffer**
Select 8 different players from the player list. These must include ONE goalkeeper, FOUR defenders, THREE midfielders and THREE strikers. **The value of your chosen players must NOT exceed £50 million.** There are no limitations on the amount of players you select from any Premiership club. If you can afford it, you can select a side made up entirely of Watford players if you wish.

2 Complete the application form, attached. Others will be published in The Daily Telegraph every Wednesday, from July 14.

3 **Now either:**
Return your completed application form, with a cheque or postal order made payable to 'Telegraph Group Limited' for £2 for each team you select to:

**Telegraph Premier League,
PO Box 4001,
Colchester CO2 8FW**
or telephone
0906 701 4 701
Calls cost 50p per minute. Average length of call is 7 minutes. Lines are open now.

How to enter a Super League
Super Leagues must include at least five teams. Select a chairman who must fill in the Super League Application Form and one Main League Application Form by following the instructions above. All the other members of the League need only complete a Main League Application Form. All Super League teams must be sent in one envelope to:
Super Leagues, PO Box 3550, Colchester CO2 8GB.
Other forms will appear in The Daily Telegraph on the dates listed above, or

you can photocopy the form in this pack (Super League's only).

Junior League All under 18s will be entered into our Junior League. Under 18s should not send cash. The cost to play is two first-class stamps to cover administration costs.

Scoring the points
The points scoring system is identical to last season.
Each Player
Appearance (full match) .... +2
Appearance (part match) .... +1
Goal scored .... +5
Key contribution to a goal .... +3
Sent off .... -5
Booked .... -2
(a player booked then sent off gets -5, not -7)

Defenders/Goalkeepers
Clean sheet (full match) .... +3
Goal conceded .... -1

Transfers Due to our revolutionary transfer system (see left) **we are now allowing 24 transfers during the season.** A maximum of 8 of these can be made by post. Your transfer cards will be included with your free and exclusive FourFourTwo magazine.

Injury Hotline
Before selecting your team, you may want to check out the latest injury news. Call **0906 36 36 906**. Calls cost 60p per minute.

Important Dates
1. There's more info on TPL forms each Wednesday in The Daily Telegraph.
2. The season kicks off on August 7.
3. Our weekly results pages are published every Wednesday from August 11.

Sparks Every team you enter will assist with the Sparks TPL medical project, aimed at preventing brain damage during labour, which is based at the University of Bristol.

Top of the league
Just like the real thing – our game is awash with cash

The TPL champion wins £25,000
The Runner-up wins £5,000
The third place manager £2,000
**The Super League
Champions share** £5,000

The Manager of the Week (most points in one week) wins £500 plus a pair of Premiership match tickets.
The Junior Champion League wins £250 voucher to spend on sports goods of their choice.
The remainder of the Top Ten Junior League managers each wins £100 of sports vouchers.

74. ITV Digital Monkey, *2001*

Imagine, if you can, the following dialogue between a puppet version of the monkey you see, and his human housemate Al, as they watch television in their living room during an advert on ITV.

Monkey: If they so much kick a ball on television it's on ITV Digital!

Al: That's not strictly true!

Monkey: DUUR, yes, it is!

Al: I bet you a million quid!

Monkey: You're on.

Al: Giggsy! [Ryan Giggs enters room wearing a maid's outfit over his Manchester United kit.]

Al: Kick that for us would yer? [Throws a football to Giggs.]

Ryan Giggs: Yes, Al. [Kicks football which bounces around room and hits monkey in the face.]

Al: Go get your monkey cheque book.

Monkey: You cheat! You knew Ryan Giggs was cleaning the stairs! [165]

Monkey is one of those rare advertising creations – a character who outlived the product he was designed to promote. A puppet monkey, he was voiced by comedian Ben Miller, the somewhat exasperated flatmate of Al, played by comedian Johnny Vegas. Monkey promoted ITV Digital's offer in between trading barbs with his flatmate, telling Al on one occasion, 'You really are the funniest man in that chair.'

Monkey outlived ITV Digital because the latter's existence was so short-lived. The company's story is also about the role of football in the fight for television subscribers and the parlous state of clubs' finances in the 2000s. Attempting to compete with BSkyB, ITV Digital paid £315 million for a three-year deal with the Football League in 2001. As the Macclesfield Town Secretary Colin Garlick later told magazine *Four Four Two*, 'Everyone pretty much said, "This sounds too good to be true." And it turned out to be exactly that.'[166] Clubs used the projected profits to plan new budgets but when the station collapsed in 2002, the successor deal was worth less than a third, leading to a run of insolvencies at Football League clubs.

ITV Digital collapsed because it failed on many levels. BSkyB's offer was better and cheaper, the equipment was inferior, and matches were scheduled at inconvenient times. Ultimately, it failed to attract enough subscribers. One report in the *Guardian* noted that a game between Nottingham Forrest and Bradford City, the rights for which cost £1.2million, attracted just 1,000 to ITV Sport. [167]

The one success was Monkey. Initially, the toys were only sent to subscribers. They proved so collectable that in one advert Monkey complained that people were trying to grab him on the street and the offer had made him 'a prisoner in my own home!'. But after ITV Digital went bankrupt, more than 32,000 entered the market as the company's assets were sold off.[168]

But this was not the end of Monkey's adventures. Firstly, he was subject to a legal dispute about who owned him – the administrators of ITV, or advertising company Mother, who had originally created him. After a brief appearance at Comic Relief in 2001, he found a new lease of live at PG Tips. Initially reunited with Johnny Vegas in 2007, in 2025 he was relaunched with a wife called Alice, played by comedian Emily Atack. Their spoof reality show, *At Home with Monkey* includes playful references to football, including Netflix's 2023 documentary *Beckham*.

'The World Amputee Football Federation was established in 2005 and the sport is now played in more than 60 countries.'

Steve Johnson's England cap

75.

Steve Johnson was a keen footballer when he had his leg amputated following an accident at the age of 21. He discovered amputee football and has accumulated a multitude of medals and awards throughout his career and beyond.

Amputee football is a game for amputees and/or people with limb-affecting deficiencies. Amputees have been pictured playing football on crutches since the early 1900s in post-war Europe. Only in the 1980s was the idea of a codified sport started, and it was formally developed by an American sports enthusiast called Dan Bennett, who lost a leg in a boating accident. He adapted the rules of traditional football for players with amputations and started the first amputee football games in Seattle. Bennett tirelessly promoted the sport and it grew rapidly in America before spreading to other nations in Europe, Africa and South America.

The first international amputee games were organised in 1984. In England, amputee football was introduced by Dr Gwynn Thomas (British Amputee Sports Association) in 1988, as a rehab activity. England sent a team to the World Cup in Seattle that same year and won gold in the indoor competition and bronze in the outdoor event. The World Amputee Football Federation was established in 2005 and the sport is now played in more than 60 countries. It is expanding rapidly, with national sides and clubs being formed all over the world and structured leagues and competitions being introduced.

Johnson, who grew up in Southport, gained 130 international caps for England and has won three World Cups. Recalling his maiden triumph, he said: 'In our first World Cup success in 1988, we came back from 3–0 down at half-time to El Salvador to win 4–3 after extra-time – very special.'[169]

Johnson was voted World Amputee Footballer of the Year in 1999 and was made the first president of the World Amputee Football Federation from 2005 to 2008. In 2019, the Disability Development Manager at Everton in the Community was awarded a Points of Light award by then Prime Minister Theresa May, recognising his outstanding contribution to the sport. He is also the Chair of the England Amputee Football Association Charity and has an active role in its junior programme.

Johnson was inducted into the National Football Museum Hall of Fame in 2008. At his induction he lent to the museum the international cap he was awarded for the 2005 World Amputee Football Federation World Championship. NFM also received one of his international shirts and a 2007 cap to tell his remarkable sporting success story as well as recognise his outstanding contribution to the growth of the sport over the past 30 years.

76. Fara Williams FA promotional card, Women's Euros, *2005*

'I just loved playing for England, I loved putting the shirt on. Didn't ever want to retire from the game, didn't ever wanna never be called up for England. I enjoyed every moment.'

Fara Williams [170]

No other Lioness has played more games for England Women than the trailblazing Fara Williams, whose 172 appearances make her the most capped player of any England team in history. The midfielder's longevity and legacy can also be seen in her 40 goals, as she is the Lionesses' joint-fourth top goal scorer of all time.

Williams' impact on the international team and women's football generally is fittingly represented in an official FA promotional card, aimed at encouraging girls and women to take up the sport. It is part of a wider set that was produced around the 2005 UEFA Women's Euros, featuring leading England women players. The main caption 'A more beautiful game' is intended to illustrate that good intentions have often come with ingrained assumptions and prejudices about how to depict and talk about female athletes.

Williams experienced homelessness aged 17 and lived in hostels for seven years after a family dispute at home. She didn't tell people at the time for fear of being judged. 'If I didn't have football, I wouldn't have got through that period,' she said. 'Living in a hostel, you see the choices some people made because they had nothing and didn't have that focus or motivation. Football saved me.' [171]

She made her full England debut on 24 November 2001, coming on as a substitute in a 1–1 away draw with Portugal. Williams went on to play at three World Cups in 2007, 2011 and 2015, and four European Championships in 2005, 2009, 2013 and 2017.

Prior to the recent achievements at the 2022 Euros and 2023 World Cup, Williams had played in the Lionesses' two best tournament results to date. She started in the 6–2 loss to Germany in the 2009 Euros final and the 1–0 victory against the same opponents in the third-place play-off game at the 2015 World Cup. It was her penalty eight minutes into extra time that made the difference.

During her club career, she was part of the Liverpool side who ended Arsenal's dominance by winning back-to-back Women's Super League titles in 2013 and 2014. She also won the Women's FA Cup twice and Women's League Cup on two occasions, in her time at Charlton Athletic, Everton and Arsenal.

After 20 years on the pitch, Williams announced her retirement from football on 26 April 2021. She played until the end of that season, but her ongoing health problems played a significant part in her decision to hang up her boots.

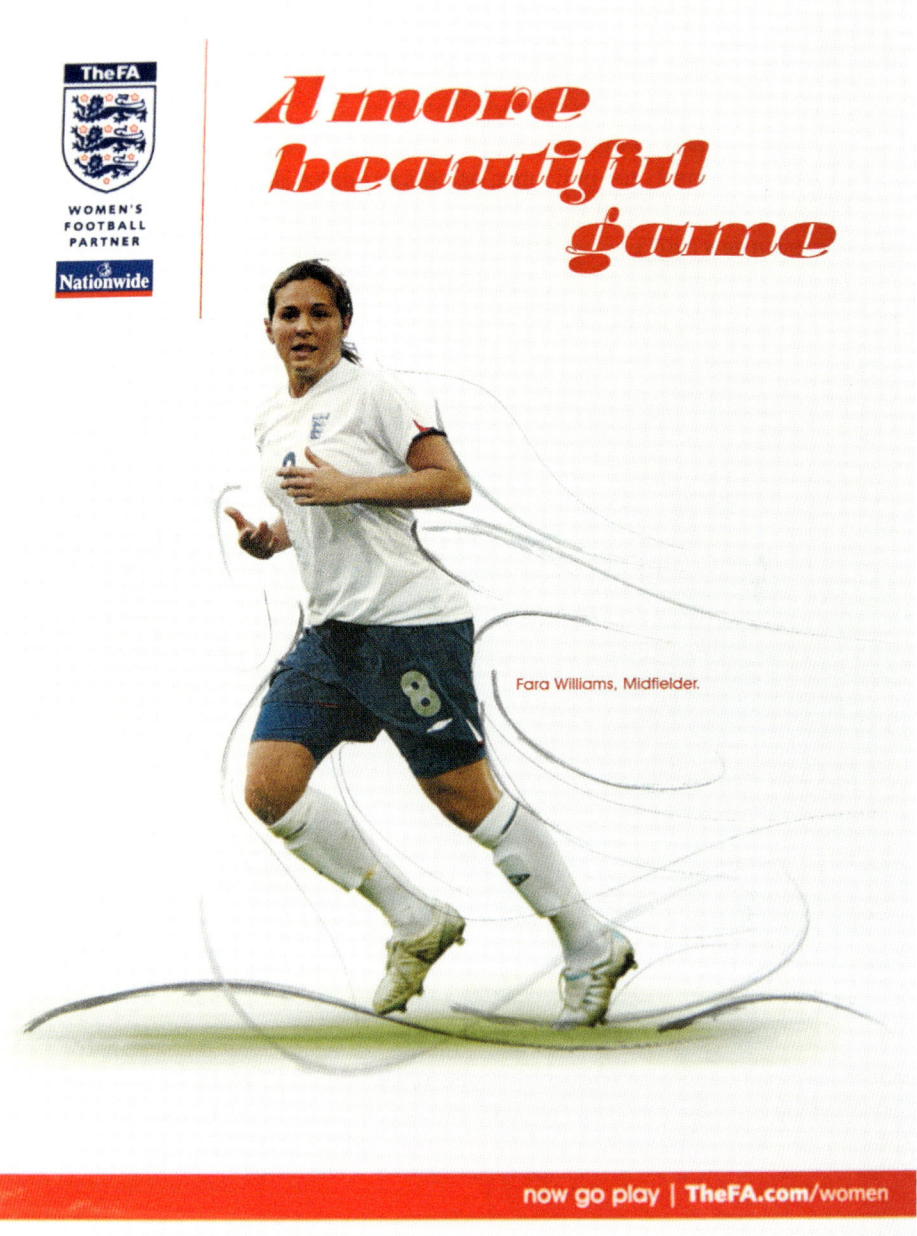

Williams played during a time of huge change in the women's game and her achievements are part of it.

'The facilities we now have, the day to day ... You know, the sports science, the diet nutritionists, the fans, media. There's so much that's changed and rightly so, and I think, you know for the right reasons and at the right pace.' [172]

77. Eni Aluko's England shirt, *2007*

'I very much feel like I'm ending on a high, with a sense that there's not much more I can do in the game.'

Eni Aluko [173]

After playing for Juventus Women and winning the Seria A, Coppa Italia and Italian Supercoppa, England centurion Eni Aluko retired from football on 15 January 2020, bringing to an end the forward's glittering playing career as she moved into executive and media roles.

Aluko was born in Lagos, Nigeria, and moved to England with her family when she was six months old. She grew up with her brother, Sone Aluko, who also became a professional footballer.

'Football was my earliest memory actually, four years old, I sort of remember kicking a football around with my little brother and we played in the local area in Birmingham,' said Aluko. 'And it was really a form of acceptance for me. There was a lot of boys in the area.' [174]

During her club career in England, she played for Birmingham City, Charlton Athletic and Chelsea, winning four FA Women's Cups, three Women's Super Leagues and other titles. Aluko also played football in the United States between 2009 and 2011, at St Louis Athletica, Atlanta Beat and Sky Blue.

After representing England at Under-17, Under-19 and Under-21 levels, Aluko made her full international debut in a 2–1 away win against the Netherlands on 18 September 2004. She played at three World Cups and finished runner-up at the 2009 Euros. Her 33 England goals make her the country's joint-seventh top goal scorer of all time.

Her England legacy is poignantly represented in the shirt she wore for her World Cup debut, in a group game against Japan, on 11 September 2007. Japan took the lead on 55 minutes through an Aya Miyama free-kick but, with time running out, England came back with two goals in two minutes through Kelly Smith. They looked to have won it but Miyama struck again with another free-kick in injury time.

'Her 33 England goals make her the country's joint-seventh top goal scorer of all time.'

It was England's first match at a World Cup in 12 years, but under head coach Hope Powell, England were gaining momentum on and off the pitch as she lay the groundwork for the future. After navigating their group, England advanced into the quarter-finals but lost 3–0 to the United States.

Since retiring, Aluko has worked in director roles at both Aston Villa Women and Angel City, and in 2024 she made history by becoming the first Black female football club co-owner. She now sits on the board of Italian team Como Women, as part of the investment group Mercury 13, who focus on the development of women's football clubs

Aluko has also utilised her platform in the media and as a pundit to vocalise issues around discrimination and diversity in the game. 'I was lucky enough to play for England 102 times,' she reflected. 'You know, Black girl from Birmingham, but I would never have been able to do that if the pathways weren't there for me to do it.' [175]

78. Hope Powell's Women's Euros medal, *2009*

'It was always about the game ... Of course, it's nice when people tell me I'm the first, but it doesn't make me any better or worse. It was just timing.'
Hope Powell [176]

Hope Powell was appointed as England Women's first-ever full-time National Coach in June 1998. At the age of 31, Powell was the youngest-ever coach of any England national football team, as well as the first woman and first non-white person to hold the position. During her 15 years in charge, she led them to two World Cup tournaments and four European Championships.

Before England Women won the Euros in 2022 and reached the World Cup final in 2023, the country's best results had been reaching the finals of the European tournament in 1984 and in 2009. Powell featured in both, firstly as a player at the first-ever Women's Euros, and then secondly as a coach.

Euro 2009 was held in Finland and it was England's sixth tournament appearance. After navigating the group stages, England beat the host nation 3–2 in the quarter-finals and the Netherlands 2–1 in the semis, to reach the final for the second time. Karen Carney and Kelly Smith both scored in the deciding game, but Germany proved too strong and won 6–2. 'We still went out to win, even at 6–2 down,' said Powell. 'We still wanted to attack, and we have to applaud that ... I think this will make the girls hungrier next time and one day it will be our day.' [177]

Between 1983 and 1998, Powell won 72 caps playing for England and scored 17 goals. She predominantly played as an attacking midfielder and made her England debut at the age of 16. She was a member of two winning England teams at the International Ladies Football Festival (better known as the Mundialito), in 1985 and 1988, which was one of the most prestigious events in women's football prior to the advent of the Women's World Cup and the introduction of the sport at the 1996 Olympics.

Powell played in the 1995 World Cup, which was England's first appearance at the tournament.

After a decade and a half of fighting to take the England Women's team and wider women's football to the next level, Powell left her role in 2013, stating she felt burnt out. However, her importance to the development of the women's game is significantly represented in her Euro 2009 final medal.

Along with all she achieved in major tournaments, she left a professional and structural legacy, after playing a key role in developing a youth system that created a clear pathway to the senior team.

'Between 1983 and 1998, Powell won 72 caps playing for England and scored 17 goals.'

Speaking about England after the historic 2022 Euros win, Powell said: 'Based on the years of hard work by so many people that came before me, so many players ... recent players that perhaps weren't involved, that to see an English team and the women's team actually win something was lovely.' [178]

'The first references to female match officials come from schoolboy games in early twentieth century.'

Amy Fearn's referee's Kit, *2010*

79.

'It felt very surreal and then started sinking in. The game stepped up a level when I entered the pitch. Going from the line to the middle is very different. There is a great relationship between male and female officials – when the referee came off he told me to stay calm and do my best.'

Amy Fearn [179]

This kit was worn by Amy Fearn when she became the first woman to referee a senior men's game in the Football League in 2010. When the original referee was injured in the 71st minute of the Championship game between Coventry City and Nottingham Forest, Fearn, as the senior assistant official, stepped in.[180] This was a historic event in the longer history of female referees in English football, one often shaped by sexism.

The first references to female match officials come from schoolboy games in early twentieth century. Male teachers were expected to referee school games, but where they were not available, female teachers stepped up. In 1919, a teacher at Ryde House School in Surrey, known only as Mrs Butler, attempted to take the referees' exam, the first step to becoming a recognised referee. However, Surrey County FA officials refused to let her take it and later decided that applications from women should not be accepted, lest they set 'a dangerous precedent.' [181]

In the decades afterwards, a handful of women managed to take the test but were never awarded the certificate allowing them to referee a men's game. This changed in 1967 when Patricia Dunn passed and then started refereeing in men's amateur football. The FA responded by introducing a ban on women being able to register as referees with county FAs. After the ban was lifted in 1976, women started to referee men's games and, in the 1990s, Wendy Toms became the first woman to be included as an assistant-official in the Football League and the Premier League. Not everyone welcomed Toms' promotion, with one Premier League official apparently saying 'it's a man's game and women don't fit in.' [182] Fearn was herself subjected to sexist comments by Luton manager Mike Newell in 2007. The Hatters boss was fined £6,500 and given a severe warning.[183]

Fearn first turned to refereeing due to a lack of playing opportunities when she was a child. Encouraged by her father, she completed a refereeing course at the age of 13 and controlled her first game at 14. While working as an accountant, her nearly 30-year career has taken in two Women's FA Cup finals, and she was also the first woman to control a first-round tie in the men's FA Cup.

After she was awarded the MBE for her services to association football in 2024, she reflected: 'It doesn't seem real at all. It's a total honour and something I never would have dreamed of really ... There were a few barriers broken down by games I've been appointed to in the past, but it has just shown there are now opportunities for everyone.' [184]

80. John Motson's sheepskin coat, 2012

'History cannot tell us whether he was wearing his trademark lucky sheepskin – all we know is that the original in a long line of lucky sheepskins spends most of its time on loan to a football museum up north – but Edgar Street, Hereford, was the day it all began for John Motson, television football commentator.

'He wasn't exactly plucked off the streets with a microphone in his hand. But after a radio apprenticeship on Sports Report, that cold, much delayed February third round replay afternoon was the moment the BBC offered Motson his small screen debut in the commentary box.

'No doubt there's an anorak out there with all the stats to hand of just how many hours of tape his unmistakable voice has filled since (in fact, probably the man himself could oblige).'

Birmingham Daily Post [185]

As football broadcasts became popular on radio and then television, the role of the commentator grew. On radio it was important to describe the action, while on television it was felt having a neutral, knowledgeable voice to add context enhanced the audience's experience. Great footballing moments became all the more entertaining and the commentator's words often became part of football folklore. The commentator became an integral part of the experience.

John Motson had been developing a career in regional radio commentary during the late 1960s before being asked to commentate on a FA Cup tie between non-league Hereford and Newcastle United for BBC's *Match of the Day*. It was anticipated to be an easy win for top-flight Newcastle, with only about three minutes of action earmarked for the flagship football highlights programme; however the game turned into one of the most dramatic giant-killing stories of the era. The cup tie ended up being the main feature on *Match of the Day* and Motson's commentary added to the excitement and drama of the day. From then on, Motson's reputation as a fact-based commentator increased and he became the regular BBC voice for big matches including the FA Cup final and World Cup tournaments.

Known affectionately as Motty, the BBC commentator became recognised for wearing this sheepskin coat. Film of him stood at football grounds across the country, often in

blizzard conditions when a game was called off, while wearing the sheepskin helped fix a 'look' for him that was impossible to shake off. Even when he went to receive his OBE from the Queen in November 2001, he was asked frequently by the media whether he'd be wearing his sheepskin for the occasion. His succinct, matter-of-fact reply was: 'I thought about it, but I didn't think it was appropriate.' [186]

Motty's preparation for any game he commentated on was immense. He'd often contact competing clubs, officials and statisticians the day before to ask in-depth questions about the players and their clubs that other reporters may have missed. He would produce a fact board for each team, packed with notes that he would use to add colour throughout his commentary.

Motson announced his retirement in 2017 after commentating on more than two thousand games for the BBC, including 10 World Cups, 10 European Championships and 29 FA Cup finals. He died on 23 February 2023, at the age of 77, after a career that had seen television football coverage grow from weekly shows focusing on two or three games, through to live games and highlights shows covering every top-flight match possible.

> 'Film of him stood at football grounds across the country, often in blizzard conditions when a game was called off, while wearing the sheepskin helped fix a 'look' for him that was impossible to shake off.'

Casey Stoney's GB Olympics football shirt, *2012*

81.

Casey Stoney, born in Basildon in 1982, was a keen footballer from a young age. On the pitch she could escape from the difficulties she faced at home. 'Football was the one place where I could go and feel free, and I could forget everything else that was going on,' she explained.[187]

Before she signed with Chelsea's academy when she was 12 years old, she played as the only girl in boys' teams, which brought its challenges: 'I got teased a lot,' she recalled. 'Back then, you had to earn their respect. The only way I could do that was by showing them what I could do with a ball.'[188] She was told girls couldn't and shouldn't play football, which made her even more determined to succeed.[189]

And succeed she did! Among her many honours are four FA Cups, three FA Community Shield and one League Cup, wins as well as being part of the England team that were runners-up in the 2009 Euros and finished third at the 2015 World Cup.

Stoney made her debut as a senior player for Arsenal in 1999 and went on to win two league titles with the club. She made her England debut in 2003 against France and represented her country at the 2007 World Cup for the first time, playing every minute of every game, until England went out in the quarter-finals against the USA. In 2012, Stoney also captained Great Britain at the Olympic Games.

The shirt in the NFM collection is from these Olympics. It was the first time there was a GB women's side competing, and the team managed by England manager Hope Powell made it to the quarter-finals, going out to Canada. Their 1–0 win in the group stages against Brazil drew a then-record crowd for a women's game at Wembley, with more than 70,000 spectators watching the match. For the Team GB kit at the 2012 Olympics, Adidas collaborated with iconic fashion designer Stella McCartney. The dark indigo blue shirt features a contemporary design inspired by the Union Jack flag.

In 2017, Stoney played her last international match for the Lionesses against France in a friendly and she retired from playing in 2018. After a stint as assistant manager for the England women's team under Phil Neville, she became the head coach for the newly formed Manchester United Women's team and led them to win the FA Women's Championship in their first season, gaining promotion to the top flight. In early 2025 she was announced as Canada's new head coach

Stoney has been an iconic figure in women's football for more than 20 years, as a player as well as manager, fighting for the right to play, equal opportunities and equal pay along the way. She is 'a strong believer that football can empower women and girls and truly be the vehicle to transform lives!'.[190]

'Stoney has been an iconic figure in women's football for more than 20 years, as a player as well as manager, fighting for the right to play, equal opportunities and equal pay along the way.'

82. Alistair Patrick-Heselton's headguard, London Paralympics 2012

'I think they should look at the beyond. I always try to educate youngsters and people in general, to be the best they can be and to understand that when one door closes another one always opens.'

Alistair Patrick-Heselton [191]

Alistair Patrick-Heselton was a talented young footballer who overcame huge adversity to rebuild his life and go on to represent Great Britain at the 2012 London Paralympic Games.

The promising schoolboy started out at Wycombe Wanderers and he was quickly signed up by Queen's Park Rangers, where he excelled as a forward at under-17 level. Patrick-Heselton made his way into the reserves team but, while on loan at Oldham Athletic, he suffered a cruciate ligament injury, which hindered his progress and development.

He played for a few semi-professional sides and decided to study for a degree in quantity surveying alongside his football career. While at Wingate & Finchley, playing in the Isthmian League, he was involved in a tragic car crash which took the life of his best friend and left him with a compound stress fracture and in a coma for two months.

'I had been told I might not walk again but I started walking towards the end of my time in hospital,' he recalled. 'I was told not to play football again and avoid contact sports full stop because of the state of my brain injury.' [192]

Four years later, he was contacted by the then Team GB Paralympic coach Lyndon Lynch, who opened the doors to a possible return to football by trying out for the England Cerebral Palsy team, consisting of players with cerebral palsy and other brain injuries. After beginning to build a new life away from football, Patrick-Heselton was hesitant, but recognising the care and attention he was shown, he gave it a go.

He made his debut at the 2011 Cerebral Palsy International Sports and Recreation Association Championships and went on to help Great Britain to the 2012 Paralympic World Cup final in Manchester. He scored to lead a fight back against Brazil but Great Britain lost the final 4–2. Only a few months later, he and Team GB competed at the 2012 London Paralympics, and during the tournament he created three assists and scored a goal against Argentina.

Patrick-Heselton's powerful journey and excellence on and off the football pitch is powerfully represented in the headguard he wore playing for Great Britain's Paralympic football team at the London 2012 Paralympic games. He wore it to prevent any fatal injuries and avoided heading the ball as a precautionary measure.

'I was told not to play football again and avoid contact sports full stop because of the state of my brain injury.'

He now works with the PFA, Premier League and reginal FAs as a mentor and speaker for the next generation of footballers, to help guide and inspire children across the country.

'The participants thoroughly enjoyed having Alistair be involved in their County Final, and that he interacted so well with the children was great! He spoke to them on a level that they understood and gave them advice to take away,' said Alex Bond of Norfolk School Games.[193]

83. Manchester United's Hillsborough tribute tracksuit, *2012*

'After the apologies, from Sheffield Wednesday then the Football Association, finally and belatedly rolled in with the Hillsborough Independent Panel's conclusive report, bereaved, vindicated families asked angrily where they had been for 23 years.

'Before the game which brought this bitter rivalry to Anfield, there was a hush in the streets outside, suggesting some emotional unity might have been forged between the clubs, too often lacking in modern football.

'Crowds assembled around the memorial at the Shankly gates to the 96 Liverpool supporters who died at Hillsborough in 1989, with its two awfully long rows of names, listed in alphabetical order from John Anderson, 62, to Graham John Wright, 17. Many Liverpool supporters touched the marble, some kissed it, before they moved away.

'Inside, the staged tributes were grand and well executed. Sir Bobby Charlton, his own life in football so overcast by Manchester United's tragedy at Munich, handed the Liverpool legend Ian Rush a bouquet of roses as a symbol of fraternity. Sir Alex Ferguson's landmark expression of solidarity with the Hillsborough families, applauding their campaign for justice, had been handed to all the United fans filing in through the Anfield Road turnstiles, just along from the memorial.

'On the pitch, the captains Steven Gerrard and Ryan Giggs released the red balloons as planned, 48 each, to let the monstrous total of 96 float up into the clouds. The sight of card mosaics displaying the words Truth and Justice, in the Kop and Centenary stands, while You'll Never Walk Alone was sung with a meaning weightier than a pop song ever intended, was great theatre of reconciliation.'

Guardian [194]

'Before the game which brought this bitter rivalry to Anfield, there was a hush in the streets outside.'

This Manchester United tracksuit remembering the 96 (since increased to 97) who died as a result of the Hillsborough disaster in April 1989 was worn prior to United's visit to Liverpool in September 2012. The game was played 11 days after the Hillsborough Independent Panel published its report, which concluded that no Liverpool fans were responsible in any way for the disaster and that its main cause was a lack of police control.

Liverpool planned to make this game with United one of commemoration and the two clubs worked together to encourage a better relationship and understanding between supporters. The volatile nature of football at the highest level had seen fans of opposing clubs use tragedy-related chants as a means of abusing their rivals. Disasters such as the Munich air crash and Hillsborough had been disrespected at times and, on this occasion, considerable effort was made to encourage a respectful tone.

This tracksuit, together with several other initiatives, did bring a more appropriate tone on the day, although in his report the *Guardian's* David Conn did highlight some isolated incidents. The game ended in a United victory but the words the *Guardian* reported from the opposing managers, Brendan Rodgers and Sir Alex Ferguson, were appropriately about the togetherness demonstrated by the fans:

Afterwards, Rodgers praised Liverpool's supporters and the pre-match tributes, saying: 'People who value human decency and humanity will have been proud today, because it's important we move on from a lot of negative stuff.' Ferguson agreed, adding: 'It demonstrates that two great clubs can unite and do these things, and then get on with the game of football with both teams trying to win.' [195]

Portsmouth FC poppy shirt, 2014

84.

Woven into this Portsmouth shirt are the names of more than 1,400 men who died serving with the 14th and 15th Battalions of the Hampshire Regiment during the First World War.[196]

It is one of many ways that British communities and organisations marked the 2014 centenary of the start of the conflict. Another club to commission a special design was Leyton Orient, who commemorated three of their players who died serving with the Footballers' Battalion. Other clubs renewed post-war memorial plaques or created new ones to remember the players and officials who served in the armed forces.

This shirt appeared in an exhibition called the 'Greater Game', the NFM's own contribution to this process of remembrance and reflection. Like all other shirts worn during games closest to Armistice Day, this also includes a red poppy. This is the symbol of the Royal British Legion and was first used in 1921. The practice of wearing the Poppy symbol on football shirts is a relatively recent one that seems to have emerged in the 2000s, with Leicester apparently the first in 2003. Its adoption on football shirts reflects the changing nature of remembrance in English football and British society.

In recent years it has brought into focus longstanding debates over whether the poppy is a neutral or political symbol. While the poppy is symbol of remembrance, it can also be seen as a show of support for the armed forces community. At international level, FIFA bans players from wearing 'political, religious or personal slogans, statements, or images'. In 2011, England and Scotland wore poppies on armbands and were fined £35,000 by FIFA. In 2016, FIFA again fined the English, Scottish, Welsh and Northern Irish FA's for including poppies on their shirts (and the Republic of Ireland for a shirt that commemorated the East Rising of 1916). The following year, FIFA relaxed its regulations around the poppy, allowing its use as long as the opposing team agrees.

At domestic level, Republic of Ireland international James McClean has faced fan and media criticism, including death threats, over his decision not to wear a poppy on his shirt while playing for English and Welsh clubs.[197] He was born in the Irish Nationalist community of Derry in Belfast, scene of the infamous Bloody Sunday massacre during The Troubles, when British troops shot and killed 13 people during a civil rights march in 1972 (a 14th person died of their injuries later). McClean has explained that as the poppy represents all of Britain's war dead, not just those who fell in the world wars, it 'represents for me an entire different meaning to what it does for others'. He added: 'Am I offended by someone wearing a poppy? No, absolutely not. What does offend me tho [sic], is having the poppy try be forced upon me.'

Today, it would be hard to imagine a major club playing without poppies on their shirts before Armistice Day. This change speaks to the continuing importance and changing nature of remembrance of military conflict in British society.

'In recent years it has brought into focus longstanding debates over whether the poppy is a neutral or political symbol.'

85. 3D model of Sergio Aguero's head, 2015

'It is really awesome working with the footballers, almost all of them do play FIFA, but only a few of them ever actually ask us about their in-game faces and stats. Overall, everyone is really excited to go through the process, of having their head scanned for the game.'

Motion Capture System Specialist Paul Boulet talking about creating the in-game likeness of footballers for the FIFA video game series, 2019

'Football players are great to work with and are very respectful. Most of them play FIFA and are usually excited to be there, which makes our job easier. We are just one small part of a very large team, so I don't think it puts any extra pressure on us.'

EA Sports Acquisition Specialist Sam Mynott, 2019

Football and video games have a long history. In the 1970s the earliest football-themed video games appeared but, like many such games of the era, the graphics were simple and match action limited. In 1979, Mattel released NASL Soccer for the Intellivision console, and this was the first football-themed game to use coloured graphics.

Atari's Pele's Soccer (also known as *Championship Soccer*) became the first licensed football game. In the 1990s, licensing deals with football's governing bodies and players became more commonplace, as did the desire to make games as realistic as possible.

This model of striker Sergio Aguero's head was made from scans created for EA Sports' FIFA game. The best-selling sports franchise video game in the world, FIFA has sold hundreds of millions of copies globally. The series was first developed in the early 1990s, with *FIFA International Soccer* (also known as *EA Soccer* and *FIFA 94*) launched prior to Christmas 1993. It quickly became a best-seller and led to the creation of *FIFA Soccer 95*, which included club teams from eight national leagues, including the Premier League. The graphics were fairly basic in comparison to modern games, with players being generic figures.

As the FIFA series developed, EA Sports invested in making the game more realistic. For FIFA 97, commentary by renowned BBC commentator John Motson was included. The following year, the graphics were improved considerably, with the offside rule also being properly implemented. By 2015, all Premier League stadia were authentically recreated, and FIFA 16 added female players. By this time, motion capture of players was being used to ensure realistic movement, with the aim of making the game as lifelike as possible.

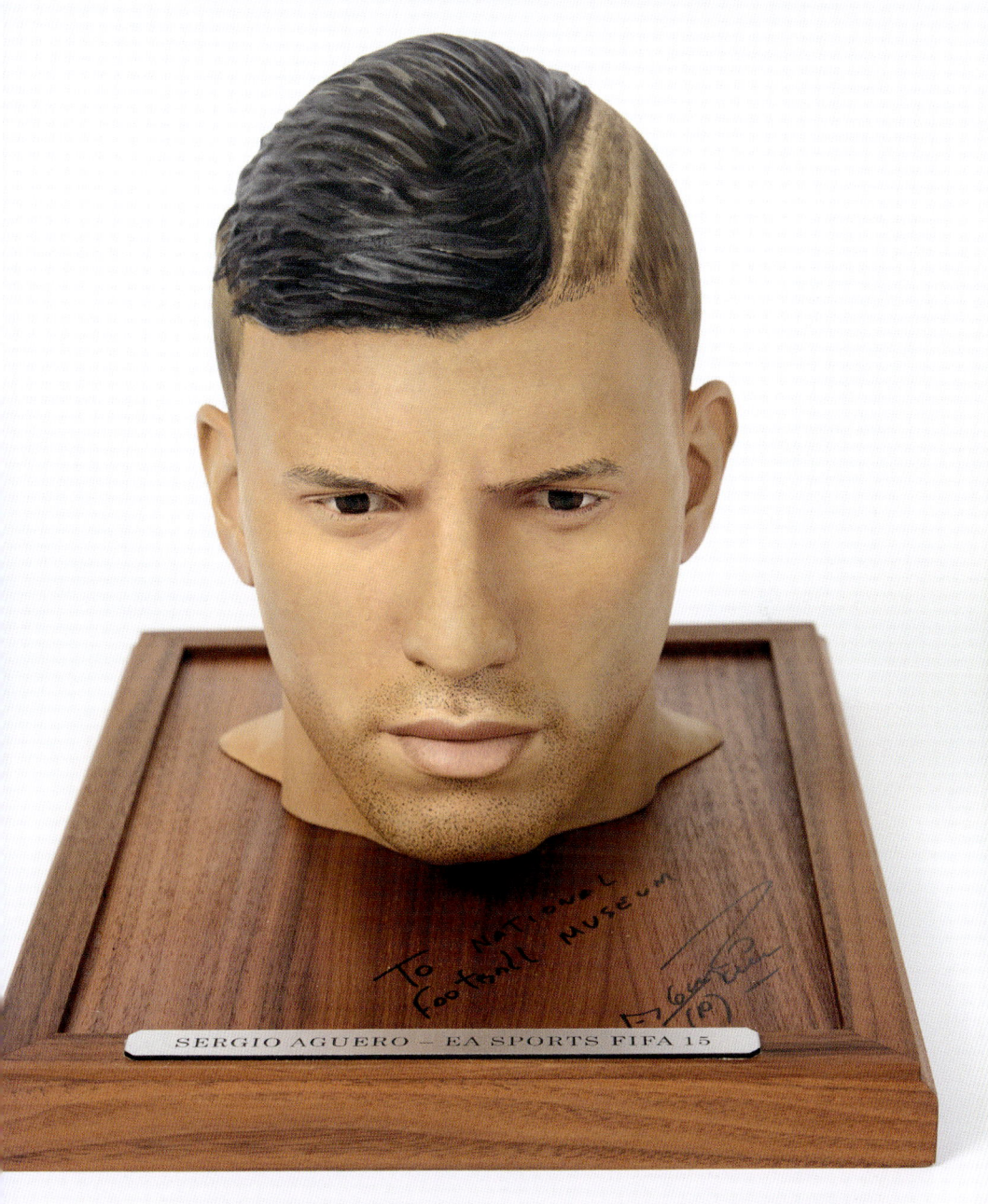

The games industry grew significantly in the 2000s, with the FIFA series growing from 16 million sales worldwide at the turn of the millennium to more than 325 million by 2021.

In 2023, the FIFA series was succeeded by a rebranded football simulation game called EA Sports FC 24. This continued to prove popular and demonstrated how football games have developed.

Stephen Daley's England shirt, 2019

86.

'At the age of 43 I now feel it is time to hand the game over to the next generation as I have left the game and the squad in a better place than when I found it in 1995.'

Stephen Daley [198]

This England shirt was worn by Stephen Daley, who represented his country 143 times during a 25-year career, 23 of which were as captain of the partially sighted futsal team. Futsal is a variant of association football, typically played five-a-side, on a smaller but harder indoor pitch like those used for basketball. Daley played in nine European futsal Championships and nine World Cup tournaments.

Born in Belfast, Daley started out with footballing aspirations, living and breathing the sport. He was part of Glentoran's youth set-up in his teenage years and earned international recognition with Northern Ireland schoolboys. However, Daley's eyesight began affecting his opportunities. He was diagnosed with cone dystrophy, a condition that affects a person's ability to pick out colour and detail. This put paid to any hopes of a professional career.

Daley began playing futsal while studying at Loughborough University, where his talent was spotted by national selectors. At the age of just 19, he featured for England at the 1995 European Championship. Daley became captain at the age of 21 and won seven international medals during his time within the England set-up, including a bronze at the 2017 Euros. Soon after, Daley led the Para Lions out at a World Cup final, losing 3–0 to Ukraine.

Two years later, a 43-year-old Daley led the Para Lions to their second successive final in Turkey, where England were once again defeated by the dominant Ukrainian side. The long-serving captain retired thereafter, having racked up 143 caps for the national side.

In 2020 Daley reflected: 'I have had a wonderful playing career and wanted to thank the FA, players and staff that have supported me along the way and given me some wonderful memories … My final game was on Saturday, 14 December 2019, as I captained England for the last time playing in the World Cup final. I owe all my achievements to the FA, the staff and players I have met along the way.' [199]

In 2020, he was awarded the MBE for services to football and futsal in the Queen's birthday honours.

After his retirement Daley put his coaching badges to good use, delivering a futsal programme with Burnley's academy. He was also appointed as head coach of the England side, helping to bring on the next generation of players following in his footsteps.

87. Lucy Clark's FA referee shirt, 2018

'Nothing's changed, I still turn up there, I'm still just the referee. The players still shout at me, the fans still shout at me. As long as they're shouting at me just because of the decisions, then that's fine. So yeah, nothings really changed, I just get on with it.'

Lucy Clark [200]

On 18 August 2018, Lucy Clark came out publicly as the world's first openly transgender football referee. She officiated her first game on the same day, in a match between QPR Women vs Parkwood Rangers.

Clark started her transition a few years before she came out as being transgender to the world. The 2017–18 season was going to be her last as a referee as she didn't think the football world would accept her, but Clark's family wanted her to continue as they knew what football meant to her. However, that Christmas, she suffered several heart attacks and was in hospital over the festive period.

'During that time, I had time to reflect and thought, hey you get one life and why should I give up something that I love, just because of who I am,' she explained. 'So, at that point I decided I was going to continue refereeing. I told the FA when I got out of hospital, and they were great. They said we don't know what to do, because you're the first, but they'll help and support any way that they can.'

Lucy Clark's journey as a trailblazer for the LGBTQ+[201] community and champion of inclusive football is beautifully represented in her referee shirt from that first game as the world's first transgender referee. 'This is the shirt, that I wore for the first ever match as my true self … crazy day.'

She is also the founder of the world's first all trans-women football club, TRUK United, and she launched Trans Radio UK, the UK's only trans radio station. On 31 March 2022, Clark and TRUK United made history by becoming the first club to field a full XI of transgender women against Dulwich Hamlet. In 2023 the club won various awards on and off the pitch, including the Football v Homophobia Grassroots Team of the Year and the Gaydio Pride Awards' LGBTQ+ Sports Team of the Year The club has also enjoyed widespread international support, with people buying the team's kit from all across the globe.

'Lots of trans, non-binary and gender non-conforming people love football,' said Clark. 'You know, it's the world's game and it's such an amazing game. It's great both physically and for your mental health as well. When you're on the football pitch, you just forget about absolutely everything else that's going on in the world. You're just concentrating on the game. As we sit here today, the women's game is so inclusive, it's fabulous. I'm honoured to be involved.' [202]

'This is the shirt, that I wore for the first ever match as my true self ... crazy day.'

88. 'Unity' the inflatable unicorn, 2022

'So, in terms of entertainment, who decides, "I'm going to pack a unicorn," for example? Whose job is that? Who's Chief Unicorn Operator?'

Gabby Logan [203]

How does an inflatable unicorn, designed for play in a swimming pool, end up as the focus of newspaper headlines, viral videos, becoming a recurring character in a newspaper cartoon, and then finally, on display in a national museum?

The inclusion of 'Unity' the inflatable unicorn might seem quirky and light-hearted, which it is, but it also reflects the growing use of psychology in the game and an important shift that took place in the relationship between the England football team, the media, and the wider public between 2018 and 2021.

After England's World Cup win in 1966, England's failures on the world stage were framed through an increasingly toxic media environment. England's failures on the field were magnified by a tabloid press that became increasingly personal and bitter in its attacks on players and managers. The nadir was probably in 1990, when the *Daily Mirror* ran a fictitious story about some of the players, to the disgust of England manager Bobby Robson.

'Jonny Sharples started a petition to have the image of defender Harry Maguire riding a unicorn featured on the new £50 note.'

Under Gareth Southgate, who took charge of the team in 2016, there was a conscious attempt to tackle this toxic past. He said: 'We always have to believe in what is possible in life and not be hindered by history or expectations.' Through the work of the team psychologist Pippa Grange and the wider FA staff, the team moved to embrace the pressure that came from playing for England.[204]

The inflatables first came to prominence at the 2018 World Cup finals. After beating Tunisia, the England players were photographed during their recovery time playing with various inflatables in the shapes of animals, including unicorns. They were a small part in a wider plan of activities and events designed not only to help the players to recover and socialise, but also to help humanise them in the media.

After the 2018 World Cup, Twitter (now known as X) meme-maker Jonny Sharples started a petition to have the image of defender Harry Maguire riding a unicorn featured on the new £50 note.[205] The unicorn also featured regularly in David Squires' *Guardian* newspaper cartoons.

The inflatables were brought out again for Euro 2020, which took place in 2021 due to the Covid-19 pandemic. This was a breakout tournament for 19-year-old Bukayo Saka, especially after footage of him jumping into a pool on a unicorn was featured on the FA's Tik-Tok account.[206] It was given to the National Football Museum by the FA in 2021 and its display made the *Big Fat Quiz of the Year* on Channel Four.

And if you are wondering about where the name came from, well, it's a nickname added by museum staff. After all, you've got to have a little fun at work now and again.

89. Lily Parr statue, *2019*

'Lily Parr was the first to put the female game firmly in the public eye, and I think it's really important that we recognise the struggles perhaps, that she had to go through, that allowed us today, to have the privilege to do what we do.'

Hope Powell [207]

This statue of Lily Parr is a rarity in the UK. While there are more than 350 sporting men immortalised in sculpture, there are only a handful of great sporting women. Statues of the male jockey Lester Piggot alone outnumber those for women.[208] At the time of writing, Parr's is the only one of a female footballer.

It was commissioned in 2019 by Mars, then an official FA sponsor, to inspire the Lionesses at that year's World Cup. Sculptured by Hannah Stewart, it was offered to the NFM and has become the centrepiece of a gallery display, funded by the Association of Independent Museums, that explores Parr's life and women's football during the era of the FA ban.

Parr is one of English football's greatest ever players and its first female superstar. Born in St Helens, she played for the most successful women's team of her time, Dick, Kerr Ladies of Preston. In 2002 she became the first woman to be inducted into the NFM's Hall of Fame.

As men fought during the First World War, Parr and other women worked in munitions factories where they seized the chance to play football. Between 1917 and 1921, the team played more than 100 games and attracted huge crowds at major stadiums. Despite the FA's ban coming into force in 1921, Parr and her teammates defiantly played on and encouraged others to do so. During her impressive 30-year career, she played across the world and scored around a thousand goals.

As part of the displays, the NFM invited women and girls to record their thoughts on what Parr's story meant to them. Former England women's manager Hope Powell was reminded of the prejudice that she had experienced.

'Having been banned myself at the age of 11 playing with the boys, being told you can't do something you love because of your gender is devastating and crushing, the question always is why, why shouldn't we have the opportunity to play this game?' [209]

Equally, Parr's story was inspiring. Thirteen-year-olds Amelie Waine and Scarlett Latta, of St Helens Girls FC, wished to emulate her by playing in front of large crowds and recognised her as a pioneer for future generations.[210]

'This statue of Lily Parr is a rarity in the UK.'

Goal Diggers FC is a trans-inclusive grass-roots football team for women and non-binary people based in London. For founder Fleur Cousens, Lily Parr's attitude chimed with her own love of football.

'She didn't take no for an answer ... and it was her way or the high-way, and I think stuff like that is great, as it shows the character that so many of us have in football ... we also play for the community you get from it and the fun which comes along with it.' [211]

90. Rashford 1 Boris 0 banner, *2020*

'This was a cry out for help from vulnerable parents all over the country and I simply provided a platform for their voices to be heard.'

Marcus Rashford

Banners and flags are a common sight in football stadiums and a vehicle for fans to support their team, show their admiration for certain players, but sometimes also to show disagreement with the club and how it is run. This banner was, however, seen tied to a street sign in Wythenshawe in Manchester rather than in a stadium. It was June 2020, and the UK had gone into lockdown in March due to the coronavirus pandemic. The football season had been suspended – the first time this had happened since the start of the Second World War. It wasn't until June when professional football started up again, but even then matches were played behind closed doors, in front of empty terraces and in silent grounds.

The banner reflected one of the game's biggest stars at the time – Manchester United forward Marcus Rashford – and a campaign close to his heart. Rashford was raised in Wythenshawe and started at United's academy system at the age of seven. At the height of the Covid pandemic he raised millions for the charity FareShare UK, helping distribute good-quality surplus food to vulnerable households. In June 2020, Rashford also campaigned tirelessly against the government's decision to not provide free school meal vouchers to vulnerable families during the summer holidays. His campaign and an open letter to the British government to end UK child poverty was credited as a turning point in forcing the government to change course.

Rashford grew up in a working-class household with a single mother working three jobs to be able to feed her family, so this campaign came from his heart having experienced the difficulties and pain a lot of families faced. He tweeted after the government's U-turn, 'Look at what we can do when we come together' and 'This was never about me or you, this was never about politics, this was a cry out for help from vulnerable parents all over the country and I simply provided a platform for their voices to be heard.'[212]

In the aftermath of this victory, local community group Wythenshawe Whispers made the banner to celebrate Rashford and to pay tribute to what a local man had achieved. The banner is in fact a cot bedsheet, with RASHFORD 1, BORIS 0 sprayed onto it in red and black paint. The banner was displayed underneath a 'Welcome to Wythenshawe' sign in the district and its picture soon went viral on social media and in the national press.

The National Football Museum had started a project in March 2020 to collect stories reflecting the effect the pandemic was having on football – its players, clubs and fans. NFM collected material ranging from clubs supporting local families with activity packs and food donations, footballers' social media messages encouraging their fans at a difficult time as well as online fitness videos, and interviews with supporters on how the lack of football was affecting them. When staff spotted the banner on social media, they quickly got in touch with the Wythenshawe Whispers group to try to collect the banner and share its amazing story. The banner was briefly stolen from the Wythenshawe sign, but after a public appeal on social media, it was returned to its creators and kindly donated to the museum.

The banner tells the story of football doing good – a footballer using his platform during the pandemic to speak out on important issues such as child poverty.

'The banner tells the story of football doing good'

91. Trent Alexander-Arnold's Black Lives Matter boots, *2020*

This is a pair of boots worn by former Liverpool right-back Trent Alexander-Arnold against Everton on 21 June 2020. The boots were made by Under Armour and feature the 'Black Lives Matter' message on one side as well as the iconic raised fist symbol on the other.

The Merseyside derby was Liverpool's first competitive game in 103 days, following the suspension of the Premier League in March because of the Covid-19 pandemic. Due to increased safety restrictions, the game was played behind closed doors, with no fans allowed inside the ground to watch. Sky had agreed to air a number of fixtures for free, and with people unable to watch in the stadium or gather in pubs, an average of five million people viewed the game at home, making it the most watched Premier League game in TV history. The match finished with a goalless draw and Liverpool had to wait until the following week to be able to celebrate their first Premier League title in 30 years.

Alexander-Arnold joined Liverpool Academy in 2004 and went through the youth teams before making his debut with the senior team in 2016. Since then he has played in two Champions League finals (winning one), won the UEFA Super Cup, FIFA Club World Cup, FA Cup, two League Cups, FA Community Shield and two Premier League titles with Liverpool.

Trent Alexander-Arnold, who moved to Real Madrid in the summer of 2025, is a footballer who uses his platform to support others and speak out on their behalf. He has been an ambassador for Liverpool-based charity An Hour For Others for many years to support underprivileged communities, and teamed up with his boot sponsors Under Armour to support doctors, nurses and other key workers during the pandemic. Together, they provided workers with more than 2,000 products at Royal Liverpool University Hospital.

Alexander-Arnold also supports the Black Lives Matter movement, which gained international attention in 2020 with global protests after the murder of George Floyd by a police officer in Minneapolis, USA. Alexander-Arnold announced that he was wearing these special pair of boots and also made a statement about racial inequality before the game: 'Tonight my boots will carry the message Black Lives Matter. It can no longer just be our feet where we express ourselves. We have to use our profile, the platforms we have and the spotlight that shines on us to say, it's time for meaningful change. The system is broken, it's stacked against sections of our society and we all have a responsibility to fix it. Black people are viewed differently. We face discrimination in actions but also in thought. It's more than just violence and abuse. Opportunity in life is restricted if you look a certain way. How can that be in 2020?' [213]

After the game the boots were given to the Nelson Mandela Foundation. More than 13,000 people donated to the raffle they organised, raising more than £27,000, and the winner of the boots was a huge Liverpool and Trent Alexander-Arnold fan. He lent the boots to the National Football Museum in 2020 to continue to tell their story and raise awareness.

'Tonight my boots will carry the message Black Lives Matter. It can no longer just be our feet where we express ourselves. We have to use our profile, the platforms we have and the spotlight that shines on us to say, it's time for meaningful change.'

Steph Houghton's Manchester City shirt, *2021*

92.

'Football means absolutely everything. To be involved in the game as a player for so long and to see the changes that we've kind of embraced over the years is unbelievable.'

Steph Houghton [214]

On the 1 May 2024, Steph Houghton played her final game, coming on as a substitute for Manchester City and taking the captain's armband in a 2–1 away win at Aston Villa Women. It brought a fitting end to a trailblazing career that lasted more than 20 years, during which time she won a vast array of major domestic honours and was widely regarded as one of the best centre-backs in the world. Houghton has led by example as captain of her club and country, and she is seen as a key figure in the transformation of contemporary women's football over the last several years.

She was scouted for Sunderland at the age of 10 and started playing first-team football at the age of 14. She went on to play for Leeds United, Arsenal and, importantly, Manchester City, where she has spent over a decade.

The Citizens' women's team, established as a City In The Community initiative in 1988, has a long and distinguished history, and on 23 January 2014, the club was relaunched and renamed as Manchester City Women's Football Club. Houghton was one of several key signings that included England internationals and promising players, such as Karen Bardsley and Jill Scott. Between 2016 and 2020, Manchester City became one of the dominant sides in English women's football.

'I think we have really set the standard and the benchmark for women's football,' she said. 'I think my highlights would probably be our first Conti Cup win in 2014. We're obviously just establishing ourselves here. We've gone from a part-time project to a full-time project and we beat Arsenal. Nobody ever really expected us to do that. We've won the league and we've won FA Cups. I've been a part of big games in the Champions League where we've come so close to reaching the finals.'

Houghton's success and longevity in the game is poignantly represented in her 150th FA Women's Super League (WSL) appearance shirt. She was wearing this jersey during a 7–1 win away at Brighton on 24 January 2021, when she became the first player to reach the milestone. During the match she scored two goals, one of which was a notable long-range dipping free-kick.

'It's a special shirt for me because this was the shirt I wore for my 150th WSL appearance,' she explained. 'It's special because I think as a footballer you want to play as many games as you possibly can and to be fortunate enough to have been involved in that many games. To score as well, it was a special day all around.'

93. European Super League protest placards, *2021*

'It felt like football fans had won for once ... on that day we stood up for a sport where ... the competition side of it had been unchanged, and we made sure it didn't get changed. I'm not naive enough to think that fans did it ... not fans on their own ... but I think that if no-one had been stood outside these stadiums and people had just rolled over, then it might have been a different story ... There were lots of things I think that stopped it ... but I do think that British fans, they made a massive effort to stop it happening ... I think that's a credit to everyone who protested against it.'

Daniel Hamilton [215]

On Sunday 18 April 2021, news was leaked that 12 European clubs would be forming a new European Super-League. (ESL) The 'dirty dozen', as they were nicknamed in the press, included six English clubs – Arsenal, Chelsea, Liverpool, Manchester City, Manchester United and Tottenham Hotspur.[216] Their proposal for a closed midweek European competition with no relegation or promotion quickly attracted opposition, ranging from fans to former players to the Prime Minister of Great Britain and the President of France. For many, it was a blatant attempt by a handful of clubs to get richer while making others poorer.

Fan opposition quickly manifested itself in protests outside club grounds. The 'Fans against Finance' placard was created by Daniel Hamilton and placed outside Elland Road before Leeds United's Premier League game with Liverpool. This was the first game after the announcement and saw Leeds United players warming up in a T-shirt that featured the Champions League logo alongside the message 'Earn it' on one side, and 'Football for the fans' on the other.

The other placard was created by Norwich City fan Ben Curtis and carried by him as he attended a protest before Chelsea's game with Brighton & Hove Albion. Part way through, news broke that Chelsea had withdrawn from the ESL and soon all but two clubs – Barcelona and Real Madrid of Spain – had followed suit.

Both placards were captured in photos that appeared in media reports across Britain and the world. Daniel's even featured in an advert by gambling company Paddy Power which saw them offer a mock 'Football Banners Helpline' for fans wanting to create one.[217] Daniel himself described how his placard 'started off as a bit of a laugh' as he scoured his girlfriend's house for suitable materials, including the tree branch from the back garden. But when he attended the protests, Daniel was struck by the unfamiliar experience of seeing fans from different clubs put aside their traditional rivalries. 'That was the most impressive thing about it,' he said.

In the long term, it remains to be seen whether the ESL idea will be resurrected. And as Daniel himself reflected, its cessation in 2021 owed much to a variety of factors, not just the reaction of fans. But arguably, April 2021 saw the voices of fans heard in a way that they are normally not. Whether this can happen again in the future is uncertain.

FOOT
BELONG,
NOT

BALL
TO US
YOU

94. Harry Kane's rainbow captain's armband, *2020*

'We're on a huge platform, on a big stage, so it is obviously a great opportunity [to wear a rainbow armband].'

Harry Kane [218]

On 29 June 2021, Harry Kane wore the rainbow-coloured captain's armband for England in a match against Germany at the Covid-delayed Euro 2020 tournament. It was done in support of LGBTQ+ communities and seen as a positive step by both Kane and the team to utilise their voice around social issues.

The rainbow armband is strongly associated with Stonewall's Rainbow Laces campaign, which was launched in 2013. Stonewall is a charity and the largest LGBTQ+ rights organisation in Europe. It was formed in 1989 by political activists to campaign against Section 28, a piece of legislation that prevented teachers from talking about same-sex relationships in schools. Stonewall was integral to the successful repeal of Section 28 in Scotland in 2000 and in the rest of the United Kingdom in 2003.

The annual Rainbow Laces campaign was created to tackle homophobia and support increasing diversity in sports across the world. Initially, rainbow laces were sent to every professional footballer in the UK for them to show their support. The armband was an extension of that, so that the captains of each side could champion the rainbow colours as part of their symbol as leaders on the pitch.

In a press conference prior to England's last-16 match against Germany in the Euros, Kane stated: 'From our point of view it is a show of solidarity with the German national team from all of us at the England national team to be united in trying to kick out all inequalities there are.' [219]

'Campaigns and actions like these are key to helping football become more accessible, welcoming and safer for everyone.'

Raheem Sterling opened the scoring for England on 75 minutes, in front of more than 40,000 people at Wembley. Then Kane took centre stage as his header in the 86th minute sealed the 2–0 win. It is a moment in history that is importantly represented in this armband as it was the first time England had beaten Germany in a knockout game since the 1966 World Cup final, as well as the first time an England captain had worn the rainbow armband.

Gareth Southgate's team may have won the game, but it was Germany's goalkeeper and captain who led the way to show support for LGBTQ+ communities at the tournament. Manuel Neuer first wore the armband in a friendly against Latvia on 7 June and continued wearing it during Germany's group stage matches. This sparked a formal investigation by UEFA, as the official rules prohibit any kind of on-field political statements from players and teams.

Europe's governing body subsequently dropped the investigation as it was assessed as a team symbol for diversity and therefore for a 'good cause'. Campaigns and actions like these are key to helping football become more accessible, welcoming and safer for everyone.

'When Marine FC of Merseyside were drawn at home against eight-time winners Tottenham Hotspur in the first round of the FA Cup in November 2020, there were 161 places between the two sides.'

Marine v Tottenham Hotspur ticket, *2021*

95.

'A Spurs fan came online … two weeks before the match, and said, "Why don't you sell online tickets, because I've seen a study in Germany." And I looked at this tweet, and I said to our Executive Director, James Leary, "Why don't we go for it?" And he organised it, and got it going, and within a few days, we'd sold 2,000 virtual tickets at £10 … and with the publicity from the match being televised, we sold 32,000 tickets.'

Barry Lenton [220]

When Marine FC of Merseyside were drawn at home against eight-time winners Tottenham Hotspur in the first round of the FA Cup in November 2020, there were 161 places between the two sides. For those looking for the romance of the cup, it was undoubtedly the tie of the round, pitching the then Premier League leaders against one from the Northern Premier League Division One North-West.

Normally, such a tie would have resulted in a bumper crowd at the 3,185-capacity Rossett Park stadium, drawn by the hope of a cup upset. But due to Covid-19 restrictions, the game took place behind closed-doors. Faced by loss of income, Marine tried to recoup some of the losses by selling virtual tickets for £10, hoping to sell about 500. Instead, they sold 32,202 tickets, principally to Tottenham Hotspur fans from 45 countries. More than £300,000 was raised, safeguarding the club's future. On the day, Tottenham won 5–0 before 9.2 million viewers on the BBC.

Clubs like Marine are true community clubs, in that they involve a great deal of voluntary support from fans and volunteers. There was additional work to be done to be ready for the 2020–21 season, with increased safety restrictions still in place. When we spoke to Community Officer Barry Lenton, he explained how he had painted 625 footprints on the terraces so fans could see where they were allowed to stand to meet social distancing protocols. Supporters were able to watch the start of their cup run in September 2020. But by the time they reached the first round proper in November, lockdowns were being reintroduced. Fans were unable to travel, with the club only allowed to bring 12 committee members on the team bus. In total, the last four games of their eight-game cup-run were played behind closed doors.

Another volunteering his time was Club Secretary and Welfare Officer Richard Cross, who fulfilled his duties on top of working in the travel industry. One of his memories of the cup-run was the 'whirlwind' of global attention the club attracted. 'We've had a lot of people around the world who adopted Marine as their second team.' He explained that the feedback from many letters and emails was that at a time when the news was full of sad stories that Marine's had cheered them, 'It's brought a smile to people's faces across the UK and across the globe.' [221]

96. Programmes marking the death of Queen Elizabeth II, *2022*

'Out of respect, the game was right to put a foot on the ball ...'
Jonathan McEvoy [222]

'It's crazy that football fans were denied a chance to pay homage.'
Martin Samuel [223]

These programmes have been collected from games that took place once football resumed after the death of Queen Elizabeth II on 8 September 2022. Her passing seems to have caught the football authorities unprepared. Before the FA could make an official pronouncement, the Premier League announced it would postpone its forthcoming weekend fixtures. In turn, the FA announced that the weekend's fixtures would be suspended across all levels of the game. In contrast, other sports like rugby union and horse racing went ahead, leading to some criticism that football had gone too far. Some grass-roots teams who went ahead with fixtures, including the prestigious public school of Eton, in turn faced criticism for failing to abide by the FA's ruling.

When Queen Victoria died in 1901, there was a similar level of controversy. The FA not only cancelled the following weekend's games across the country but also the scheduled FA Cup fixtures after that, and urged clubs to cancel any other matches due to the Queen's funeral. However, Football League clubs were angered by the unilateral cancellation of games and disruption to their schedules. On the first weekend, several clubs, including Manchester City, Newton Heath (later Manchester United) and Woolwich Arsenal, defied the FA by playing. Following this, there were fears that games would be played on the day of the Queen's funeral, but eventually tempers cooled and no fixtures went ahead.

In contrast, the deaths of King George V in 1936 and King Edward VI in 1952 saw a more unified approach. In both cases the FA decided, after discussions with the Lord Chamberlain's Office, that it was more appropriate to let football continue, except on the date of the King's funeral. The FA also guided its clubs on expected forms of mourning which were to include black armbands to players, playing the hymn Abide with Me (through live bands or records), holding a minute's silence, and then playing the national anthem. These allowed players and fans to come together in striking moments of collective mourning, as newspaper photographs at the time demonstrate.

Whereas the design of early matchday programmes allowed for relatively little reference to the passing of earlier monarchs, these modern covers capture some of the different ways that clubs interpreted the Queen's death. Tottenham Hotspur and Leeds United were among those depicting her presenting the FA Cup to their victorious captains. Others without such prestigious connections used official photographic portraits, most often in black-and-white, but in some cases using a colour portrait from her Coronation in

> 'When Queen Victoria died in 1901, there was a similar level of controversy.'

1953. Inside, editorials, chairmen and managers all paid their respects, stressing her long service to the nation and her personal qualities. Some included additional content, such as former players recalling meeting with her, or photo montages of royal visits. Of those the National Football Museum collected, only one acknowledged that, 'not everyone is a supporter of the monarchy as a system.' [224]

97. Ellen White's boots, *2022*

'This decision has always been one I have wanted to make on my terms. And this is my time to say goodbye to football and watch the next generation shine.'

Ellen White [225]

On 22 August 2022, Ellen White announced her retirement from football. It brought to an end her 17-year playing career, in which she starred as a forward for some of the top English clubs in women's football.

White's goal-scoring legacy is fittingly represented in the Adidas Predator 'Edge' boots that she wore in her final Women's Super League appearance on 8 May 2022. The club did not know it yet, but it was the last time White would play for Manchester City, and she signed off her club career in style heading in City's third goal from a corner, as they beat Reading away 4–0.

Later that year, after winning the Euros with England, she chose to hang her boots up on a career high. 'To kind of end my career on winning a Euros was just the most special moment ever really, it was just amazing.' [226]

'To kind of end my career on winning a Euros was just the most special moment ever really, it was just amazing.'

White was born and raised in Aylesbury and came through the academy at Arsenal. In 2005, at the age of 16, started her career at Chelsea Women FC and was their top scorer for three consecutive seasons. She went on to join Leeds Carnegie but, a few months after signing, she suffered a cruciate ligament injury that kept her sidelined for a long spell. In her second campaign she hit a season total high, grabbing 18 goals in 26 appearances overall.

Between 2010 to 2013, White was part of a dominant Arsenal side who won numerous titles and cups. In 2011, her most prolific goal-scoring season for the club, she helped them win a domestic treble of the Women's Super League, FA Cup and League Cup. During her time playing for Birmingham, she won the WSL Golden Boot in 2017–18, scoring an impressive 15 goals in 14 appearances.

White moved to her final club, Manchester City, in 2019, where she won her final piece of domestic silverware. They beat Chelsea 3–1 in the 2022 League Cup final and she scored the second goal with a close-range poacher's finish.

White made her international debut against Austria in March 2010 and went on to make 113 appearances for England. In 2021, she had her best international scoring return with 12 goals in nine appearances. She played an important role in England's historic 2022 European Championship win, by starting all six games and scoring twice in the 8–0 victory over Norway. She also signed off with a record 52 goals for the national team.

'It has been my greatest honour and privilege to play this game,' she said. 'Playing for England has and always will be the greatest gift.' [227]

'It has been my greatest honour and privilege to play this game … Playing for England has and always will be the greatest gift.'

98. Nikita Parris's Euros medal, 2022

'Football helps me express myself. When I am out there on the pitch nothing else matters.'

Nikita Parris [228]

On 3 July 2022, England made history by beating Germany 2–1 in the European Championship final. Ella Toone had scored a sublime chip to open the scoring, but Germany equalised through Lina Magull and the game went into extra time. The winner came through Chloe Kelly, who poked home the ball from close range after a scramble in the box. Nikita Parris came on as a substitute in extra time as the Lionesses held out for the historic win. It was the first major footballing tournament England had won in 56 years and the first such success for the women's team.

The increased focus and hype around the tournament were in tune with a growing public interest in women's football and England did not fail to deliver. The Lionesses were unbeaten in the group stages, scoring 14 goals and conceding none. They only shipped two goals during the whole tournament and finished up scoring 22 goals in all.

Parris was born in Toxteth, Liverpool, and grew up supporting the Reds but through her school teachers' influence, her own career started at city rivals Everton. 'I think my biggest inspirer was my school teacher,' she explained. 'He actually believed in me when I was probably eight years old and saw talent in me that I didn't actually see myself. He was the one who pushed me to go to his favourite team, which was Everton. I supported Liverpool, but he believed in the pathway that Everton provided … He believed, yeah, I could reach the top of the game.' [229]

Since leaving Everton, she has gone to play for some of the biggest and most successful clubs in women's football, most notably Manchester City, where she won several trophies, including the domestic treble in 2016. She then moved to Olympique Lyonnais Féminin, where she won the Champions League in 2020. She most recently won the FA Cup again with Manchester United 2024, before moving to Brighton and Hove Albion.

Parris's journey to the top of the women's game is significantly represented in her European Championship winners' medal from 2022. Since Parris made her senior international debut in 2016, she has made more than 70 appearances and played an important role in England's growing success in recent years. She has scored 17 goals for her country, which include scoring at the Euros in 2017 and the World Cup in 2019.

'When I look at it, I see so many emotions,' she said. 'The ups and downs of football, of what it takes to reach the pinnacle. Most of all I feel relief that I achieve something I have always dreamed about.' [230]

'The increased focus and hype around the tournament were in tune with a growing public interest in women's football and England did not fail to deliver.'

99. Mary Earps's WSL Manchester United shirt, *2022*

'I hate conceding goals. If I could have my way, I wouldn't let a single goal in ever again.'

Mary Earps [231]

Mary Earps currently plays for Paris Saint-Germain and is regarded as one of the best goalkeepers in the world. She played every minute for England at the Euros in 2022, helping them beat Germany 2–1 in the final and win the tournament for the first time. She only conceded twice and kept clean sheets in four of the six games.

She has won a host of high-profile individual awards, including back-to-back wins of The Best FIFA Women's Goalkeeper award in 2022 and 2023. 'I am just blown away,' she reflected. 'I talk a lot obviously about how it hasn't been an easy journey. Some would say I took the scenic route. But it made me feel so much prepared for the challenges ahead.'[232] In 2023 she also won the World Cup Golden Glove, as her three clean sheets helped England reach the final for the first time.

Her goalkeeping achievements and pedigree are appropriately represented in her Women's Super League (WSL) 50th clean sheet appearance shirt. She was wearing this jersey when she achieved the milestone and helped Manchester United beat Reading Women 1–0 on 22 January 2023. Just before Rachel Williams scored the late winning goal, Earps produced a big save to keep the score level, by tipping a Justine Vanhaevermaet header around the post. She was the first goalkeeper in the league's 12-year history to achieve 50 shutouts and, that season, she also went on to win the 2022–23 WSL Golden Glove, by setting a new record of 14 clean sheets.

Earps had to be patient and work hard for her England chance by competing with the likes of Karen Bardsley and Carly Telford. She made her international debut on 11 June 2017 in a 4–0 friendly win over Switzerland in Biel. She went on to gain more caps but, after playing against Germany in November 2019, she would have to wait nearly two years before representing her country again.

Earps has stated that in early 2021, she considered moving away from football as her United contract was coming towards an end, getting back into the England team seemed unlikely, and she had other interests to pursue. This moment would prove to be a turning point in both her club and international career.

'Earps made her international debut on 11 June 2017 in a 4–0 friendly win over Switzerland in Biel.'

After signing a contract extension at United, she would go on to help them to finish second in the WSL in 2023 and win the FA Cup the following year. For England, Sarina Wiegman became the head coach and reignited her international career. Earps regained her place in an 8–0 win over North Macedonia on 17 September 2021 and went on to make history with the Lionesses, before calling time on her England career ahead of Euro 2025

'For anyone who has ever been in a dark place, just know that there's light at the end of the tunnel,' she said. 'Keep going, you can achieve anything you set your mind to.' [233]

100. Leah Williamson's Finalissima England shorts, *2023*

'We work hard, we put the work in, we don't shy away. We give everything we can to England in this pursuit of this greater goal, but we're gonna enjoy it along the way.'

Leah Williamson [234]

On 6 April 2023, England's captain Leah Williamson helped the country follow up on their historic Euros triumph by beating Brazil to win the inaugural Women's Finalissima at Wembley. The game was not just significant for the cup win, as it was also the first time the Lionesses had worn a new England home kit, which included design elements in response to the players' feedback.

Set against the 50-year ban the FA placed on women's football in 1921, the women's game has suffered in numerous ways. This includes the kit that has been available to them and its overall design. In the past, much of it has been designed for men and even now, the consideration of different female needs is only just emerging.

After some of the England players raised concerns about the all-white kit they wore during the 2022 Euros, the manufacturer Nike changed the next kit's shorts to blue. The shorts feature a leak-protection liner to help make players on their periods feel more comfortable about playing and performing in public.

'When we showed them this innovation, they told us how grateful they were to have this short, to help provide confidence when they can't leave the pitch,' said Jordana Katcher, vice-president of Nike women's global sport apparel. [235]

We are now slowly seeing the increased input from female footballers in modern kits and more recently the design of boots. Nike's 2023 Phantom Luna boot put the female foot at the forefront of its technology, taking into account the growing number of ACL injuries in the game.

> **'After some of the England players raised concerns about the all-white kit they wore during the 2022 Euros the manufacturer Nike changed the next kit's shorts to blue.'**

The first Women's Finalissima was an intercontinental cup match, between England as the winners of the 2022 Euros, and Brazil as winners of the 2022 Copa América Femenina. England were heading to victory, via a cut-back from Lucy Bronze and a sweeping strike from Ella Toone, but lacklustre defending and a Mary Earps spill led to Brazil's Andressa Alves' injury-time equaliser.

The game went to penalties and Earps made up for her earlier mistake with a crucial save to keep Tamires out. England were clinical and won the shootout 4–2, with Chloe Kelly scoring the decisive spot-kick. The win also extended their impressive unbeaten run to 30 games.

'Every time you win, it makes you wanna win more,' said Williamson. 'Those penalty takers are incredible for us, Mary we know how good she is in goal as well. I weren't worried at all.' [236]

Building on the Euros and Finalissima successes, England again created history by reaching the 2023 World Cup final. Unfortunately, they narrowly lost the game 1–0 to Spain, but this talented group of England players have been at the forefront of success, empowerment and change in the women's game.

'I picked it up and tore some paper and saw a woman holding a dish over her head, and disks with the words Germany, Uruguay, Brazil. I rushed inside to my wife [and] said, "I've found the World Cup! I've found the World Cup!"'

Pickles' collar, *1966* 101.

Each of the 100 objects in this book so far are fascinating and unique, and together we hope they've told a powerful and inclusive story of the game we all love so much. But there's one particular piece in the National Football Museum's collection with a story so extraordinary, we couldn't resist including here at the end.

Pickles the dog was one of the heroes of the 1966 World Cup in England – off the pitch! When the Jules Rimet Trophy was stolen in March 1966 at the Stampex exhibition in the Westminster Central Hall in London, Pickles saved England and the FA a lot of embarrassment by sniffing out the missing silverware only a week later.

Pickles, a black and white mixed breed collie, lived with his owner David Corbett in Norwood, South London. Corbett had taken Pickles off his brother John as a puppy four years earlier. They left their home on 27 March 1966, as David Corbett needed to make a call from the phone box opposite his house, when Pickles went over to a parked car and started sniffing at a package near the front wheel. Corbett, who at first thought it was a bomb, carefully tore open some of the newspaper: 'I picked it up and tore some paper and saw a woman holding a dish over her head, and disks with the words Germany, Uruguay, Brazil. I rushed inside to my wife [and] said, "I've found the World Cup! I've found the World Cup!"' [237]

Corbett rushed to the nearest police station and was promptly treated as the prime suspect. He was detailed for questioning but later cleared as he had an alibi. Pickles became a superstar once the story got out, he even knocked Harold Wilson and the general election that week off the front pages of the newspapers in the morning. Pickles was made Dog of the Year, received a year's worth of free dog food and appeared on many TV programmes, for instance *Blue Peter* and *Magpie*. Pickles even starred in the comedy film *The Spy with the Cold Nose* with Eric Sykes later that year. He also received many other rewards such as this collar, which features a little plaque engraved with his name and two small medallions, one from the Canine Defence League and the other from the World Cup Collectors' Club.

David Corbett received £3,000 as reward money, which enabled him to buy a house in Surrey. Sadly, Pickles' luck ran out the year after when he chased a cat up a tree and was strangled by his choke-chain. Corbett buried him at the end of his garden. The Jules Rimet Trophy, which brought Corbett and Pickles their fame and rewards, was stolen again in 1983 and never recovered. The story of Pickles the dog and how he saved the World Cup is still fondly remembered around the world to this day. His collar was kindly lent to the National Football Museum courtesy of David Corbett.

Epilogue
What the National Football Museum does and why

Traditionally, museums have led on what objects they choose to collect and preserve as they record and interpret the world around them. Experts in curation, conservation, registration and documentation make acquisition decisions based on their knowledge and experience to continually develop a museum's collection. This is an integral part of a museum's ecosystem as it looks to build on existing narrative strands and strengths within its collection, while also beginning new ones to represent and document changes in society and culture.

Museums can effectively draw on their internal resources to decide on how to record what is happening around them, but this can be complemented with a wider arms-open approach to contemporary collecting. Instead of the museum solely looking outwardly at the world and bringing material in, it invites the outer world in to help choose what it acquires. It can do this by using its credentials to engage with local and national communities to help shape how we capture and represent life for the people of today and the people of tomorrow.

Over the last few years, the National Football Museum has continued to utilise its expertise to collect but it has also pursued contemporary collecting through community consultation and co-curation. We have worked with footballers, managers, referees, fans, campaigns and organisations to help us shape decisions about what elements of football history to collect, and what objects and stories matter to people. Working in tandem with

Museums can effectively draw on their internal resources to decide on how to record what is happening around them, but this can be complemented with a wider arms-open approach to contemporary collecting.

the wider football community is vital to fulfil the museum's aim of telling a representative story of the nation's favourite game so everyone can explore why football matters.

Part of the approach is to document people's voices along with the objects, so we can platform their opinions and experiences. We do this through collecting written quotes or filmed interviews and conversations with donors or wider people and communities connected to the objects. This model provides the newly acquired objects with attached organic personal histories, giving them more authenticity and humanity.

Some of the most focused contemporary collecting through community consultation and co-curation has been centred on historically under-represented areas in our collection. This has been pursued as part of a long-term engagement strategy so the collecting we do delivers real impact and builds meaningful connections to the people involved and wider communities.

One of the largest areas of recent contemporary collecting has been in top-level women's football. By building relationships with leading clubs the Women's Super League (WSL), which included Arsenal, Chelsea, Manchester City and Manchester United. We invited them to co-curate an object into the collection and engage their players in representing the story of their club today.

At a time of exponential growth in the women's game, this strand of contemporary collecting has since developed even further.

Here's Scottish international Erin Cuthbert on the item she gave us: 'I am donating a used pair of my Adidas boots. Scored many a banger in these. Many amazing memories. A lot of blood, sweat and tears are coming into the museum. So, yeah, it's an honour for me.'[238]

At a time of exponential growth in the women's game, this strand of contemporary collecting has since developed even further. The museum now works with the Football Association to do a similar sort of thing and benefits from their wider reach to other clubs in the WSL and Women's Championship.

Another important contemporary collecting strand has been to develop our links and engagement with football's LGBTQ+ communities. We have continued to consult and co-curate with inclusive football clubs, initiatives and individuals. These have included Manchester Laces, Just a Ball Game? Manchester City, Lucy Clark and Blair Hamilton. For instance, in 2022, as part of the club's Rainbow Laces celebrations, Manchester City donated a pride flag signed by players across the men's and women's 2021–22 squads.

The Black in the Game exhibition opening in 2025 focused on the experiences of African and Caribbean communities in football. Part of that project's aim has been to similarly forge relationships with clubs by consulting and co-curating some of the stories of their players today. These have included Fulham, Everton, West Ham and Chelsea. Here's Bobby De Cordova-Reid: 'This is a shirt from the Gold Cup, my first Gold Cup tournament for Jamaica. That was in America, a couple of years back. It means quite a bit to me. Obviously, it's one of the first shirts that had my name on the back, and obviously being the 10 shirt as well means a lot. As an iconic jersey for Jamaica, I'm happy to be donating it.'[239]

There are other areas and communities too numerous to mention here that the museum has engaged in this way as it looks to represent and platform a collection of diverse experiences. Football is a team sport and by its nature should and can be inclusive, and our contemporary collecting must reflect that.

Acknowledgements

The National Football Museum would like to thank the team involved in the creation of this work. The objects featured here come alive thanks to your creative storytelling. Thanks to Wiebke Cullen, Dave Edwards, Dr Alexander Jackson, Marek Romaniszyn and Dr Gary James.

Thanks, too, to Jon Shard for the beautiful object photography featured in this book.

We'd also like to thank the following organisations and individuals for the loan of their objects to the Football Heritage Collection, and that are featured in this book:

The Priory Collection for objects *18, 28, 34, 37*
The Football Association for objects *3, 33, 59*
The Players Foundation for objects *16, 20, 46*
The EFL for object *9*
The Lancashire FA for object *7*
Manchester City for object *17*
Brian Finney for object *36*
The Collins Family for object *39*
Rachel Robinson for object *40*
Andrew Leslau, RAM and The Priory Collection for object *43*
The Virgin Group, the Eurostar group and The Mirror group for object *44*
Gill Sayell for object *48*
Liz Deighan for object *51*
Viv Anderson for object *52*
Angela Gallimore for object *53*
The Hillsborough Family Support Group for object *55*
Jeff Maysh/The Lilywhite Collection for object *63*
Arsenal FC for object *64*
Robbie Fowler for object *68*
Stuart Roy Clarke for object *69*
Steve Johnson for object *75*
Hope Powell for object *78*
Rob Lingham for object *91*
Nikita Parris for object *98*

Finally, the museum would like to thank everyone at HarperNorth for their support, especially Jon De Peyer for your guidance and encouragement. We're pleased to be able to explore the uniqueness of our collection and the expertise of our curatorial team through storytelling and demonstrate the ways in which football matters.

Endnotes

1. Except photographs of objects 15, 19, 31 and 69.
2. Tony Collins, *How Football Began: A Global History of How the World's Football Codes Were Born*. 2018
3. Ibid., pp.4–9.
4. *Bell's Life in London & Sporting Chronicle*, 17 October 1863.
5. Collins, p.8.
6. Collins, p.36.
7. Jean Williams, *The Girls of the Period Playing Ball: The Hidden History of Women's Football, 1869–2015*, 2017.
8. Bunk, B. (2021), *From Football to Soccer: The Early History of the Beautiful Game in the United States*. 1st edn. Champaign: University of Illinois Press.
9. Ibid.
10. Ibid.
11. Ibid.
12. Graham Curry, 'Football in the capital: a local study with national consequences', Soccer & Society, 24 July 2017.
13. Howson, E.W. & Warner, G.T. (eds), *Harrow School*, 1898.
14. Unknown author, (1871) 'Wanderers v Harrow School', *Bell's Life in London*, 11 February.
15. http://englandfootballonline.com/seas1872-00/1872-73/m0001sco1872.html
16. http://englandfootballonline.com/seas1872-00/1872-73/m0001sco1872.html
17. Unknown author. (1882) 'The East Lancashire football charity cup', *Blackburn Times*, 20 May.
18. Unknown author. (1895) 'Feminine footballers', *Sketch*, 6 February.
19. Tom Brown's Schooldays was hugely influential in encouraging the spread of Rugby Football. See *Tony Collins, A Social History of English Rugby Union* (London: Routledge, 2009).
20. All information based on 'The Father of Football Fiction? A.S. Hardy and the popularisation of Association Football fiction in the Boys' Story Papers of the Amalgamated Press, c1900–1939' by Alexander Jackson, *Sport in History*, Vol.42. Number 1, March 2022.
21. *Boys' Realm Sports Library*, 22 February 1913.
22. Steve Tait, 'Edward Hulton and sports journalism in late-Victorian Manchester', in *Sport in Manchester*, edited by Dave Russell (2009).
23. Paul Joannou, *United – the First 100 Years: The Official Centenary History of Newcastle United* (1992).
24. A named Cyclops from Homer's *Odysseus*.
25. *Athletic News*, 22 April 1910.
26. NFM Collections, FIFA T1.2.
27. John Harding, *Football Wizard: The Billy Meredith Story. The Life and Times of Football's First Superstar* (London: Robson Books, 1998).
28. *Topical Times*, 19 April 1930.
29. James, G. (2010) *Manchester a football history*. Halifax: James Ward.
30. Margaret Timmers, *A Century of Olympic Posters* (London: V&A Publishing, 2008).
31. All information about the tournament is from Steve Menary, *GB United?: British Olympic football and the end of the amateur dream* (Durrington: Pitch Publishing, 2010).

32 Menary.
33 Andrew Riddoch and John Kemp, *When the Whistle Blows: The Story of the Footballers' Battalion in the Great War* (CreateSpace Independent Publishing Platform, 2015). All information about the battalion is from this source.
34 Andrew Riddoch and John Kemp, *When the Whistle Blows: The Story of the Footballers' Battalion in the Great War* (CreateSpace Independent Publishing Platform, 2015). All information about the battalion is from this source.
35 Tony Collins, *A Social History of Rugby Union* (London: Routledge, 2009).
36 Riddoch and Kemp.
37 Gavin Mortimer, *Fields of Glory: The Extraordinary Lives of 16 Warrior Sportsmen* (London: Andre Deutsch, 2001).
38 All information about Donald Simpson Bell's military career drawn from Mortimer.
39 https://www.nam.ac.uk/explore/victoria-cross (Accessed: 7 March 2025).
40 https://www.footballandthefirstworldwar.org/donald-bell/ (Accessed: 7 March 2025).
41 Mortimer.
42 *Bath Chronicle*, 21 April 1928.
43 *Bath Chronicle*, 31 July 1915 and 23 August 1919.
44 Unknown author. (1919) 'The sports girls of Paris', *Evening News*, 1 November.
45 Unknown author. (1932) 'Women's football: International match for Sheffield', *Daily Independent*, 23 July.
46 This chapter is based on https://www.donmouth.co.uk/womens_football/stoke_ladies.html and https://www.donmouth.co.uk/womens_football/elfa.html accessed 20.2.2025.
47 Tiller, M. (2025) *England Came Knocking – But Then The Door Slammed Shut*. Available at: https://jackleslie.co.uk/jack/# (Accessed: 20 March 2025).
48 Johnes, M., Jackson, A. (2019) *Jack Leslie: The man who should have been England's first black international footballer*. Available at: https://martinjohnes.com/2019/10/02/jack-leslie-the-man-who-should-have-been-englands-first-black-international-footballer/ (Accessed: 20 March 2025).
49 BBC (2021) *Jack Leslie: Statue sculptor for black footballer* chosen. Available at: https://www.bbc.co.uk/news/uk-england-devon-57682335 (Accessed: 20 March 2025).
50 Brown, P. (2018) *Hell for leather: Mystery surrounds the first ever World Cup final ball* [Online]. Available at: https://www.wsc.co.uk/stories/hell-for-leather-mystery-surrounds-the-first-ever-world-cup-final-ball/ (Accessed: 01 March 2025)
51 Stanley Matthews, *Feet First* (London: Ewan & Dale, 1948), pp.86-7.
52 Alexander Jackson, *Football's Great War: Association Football on the English Home Front, 1914–1918* (Barnsley: Pen & Sword, 2021).
53 Peter Beck, *Scoring for Britain: International Football and International Politics, 1900–1939* (London: Routledge, 1999).
54 Ibid.
55 London Seawood FC, 10 March 2023. https://x.com/LondonSeawardFC/status/1634280889524932610 (Accessed: 20 March 2025).
56 *Leicester Mercury*, 13 May 1939, *Daily Herald*, 15 May 1939.
57 All information about Frank Soo from Susan Gardiner, *The Wanderer: The Story of Frank Soo* (Stowmarket: Electric Blue Publishing, 2016).

58 https://nationalfootballmuseum.com/news/frank-soo-hall-of-fame/ (Accessed: 28 February 2025).
59 Unnamed newspaper clipping, Margaret Melling Collection. PRSFM: 2023.163.33.
60 https://www.britishpathe.com/asset/94969/ (Accessed: 7 March 2025).
61 Norman Baker, 'Have they Forgotten Bolton? The Sports Historian', No.18, 1, (May 1998).
62 https://www.playingpasts.co.uk/articles/gender-and-sport/nellie-halstead-once-known-as-britains-greatest-women-athlete/ (Accessed: 7 March 2025).
63 https://www.sthelensstar.co.uk/news/1520106.peggy-was-the-rock-in-defence/ (Accessed: 7 March 2025).
64 https://collectingartfootball.wordpress.com/2015/04/15/gerald-cains-on-saturday-taxpayers-1953/ (Accessed: 11 March 2025).
65 Ray Physick, 'The Representation of Association Football in Fine Art in England from its Origins to the Present Day,' Unpublished PhD. University of Central Lancashire, 2013.
66 https://collectingartfootball.wordpress.com/2015/04/15/gerald-cains-on-saturday-taxpayers-1953/ (Accessed: 11 March 2025).
67 http://news.bbc.co.uk/1/hi/uk/545023.stm (Accessed: 11 March 2025).
68 Physick.
69 Joyce Woolridge, 'From local hero to national star?': The changing cultural representation of the professional footballer in England, 1945–1983. Unpublished PhD, University of Central Lancashire, 2007.
70 See Billy Wright, *Captain of England* (1950), *The World's My Football Pitch* (1953), *Football is My Passport* (1957) and with Bryon Butler, *One Hundred Caps and All That* (1962)
71 https://www.wolves.co.uk/news/club/20210226-graham-hughes-1933-2021/ (Accessed: 17 February 2025).
72 All information about Pegasus and the FA Amateur Cup from Dilwyn Porter, 'Amateur Football in England, 1948–1963: The Pegasus phenomenon,' in Contemporary British History, 14:2, 2000.
73 Brian Hunt, *Northern Goalfields Revisited: The Millenium History of the Northern Football League* (Shildon: Masterprint, 2000).
74 For British referees in South America, see *Tony Mason, Passion of the People?: Football In South America* (London: Verso, 1995). In Argentina, see David Downing, *England v Argentina: World Cups and Other Small Wars* (London: Portrait, 2003). For Brazil, see Aidan Hamilton, *An Entirely Different Game: The British Influence on Brazilian Football* (London: Mainstream Publishing, 1998).
75 IF: *The House Journal of Imperial Foods Limited*, No.18. June 1976.
76 Findley, R. (1954) 'Finney splits the cash with his team-mates', *Daily Express*, 1 May.
77 James, G. (2008) 'Manchester remembers', *Manchester Evening News*, 2 February.
78 James, G. (2025) *Manchester Corinthians: The authorised history*. Halifax: James Ward.
79 https://www.bbc.co.uk/sport/football/55987450 (Accessed: 20 March 2025).
80 Elizabeth Taylor Collection.
81 The NFM holds a copy. See PRSFM: 2017.969.
82 All quotes and information taken from an account of Elizabeth's life provided by Trizia Wells to the NFM.
83 Sheffield Green'Un, 4 March 1980.
84 Birmingham Sports Argus, 14 October 1961.
85 Simon Inglis, *The Football Grounds of England and Wales* (London; Willow Books, 1983).

86 *Daily Mirror*, 12 November 1962.
87 See Matthew Taylor for a clear summary of the academic debate over hooliganism in *The Association Game: A History of British Football* (London: Routledge, 2008), pp.310-19.
88 https://www.bbc.co.uk/news/uk-england-27490920#:~:text=They%20were%20formed%20by%20high,and%20Kop%20ends%20in%201977 (Accessed: 13 March 2025).
89 Classic Football Matches + (2023) 1971 - THIS IS YOUR LIFE (Bobby Moore). 9 January. Available at: https://www.youtube.com/watch?v=RoLNQbWPmGg (Accessed: 10 March 2025).
90 History of Football (2016) ENGLAND 1966 WORLD CUP FINAL Victory As Told By Sir Bobby Charlton. 25 February. Available at: https://www.youtube.com/watch?v=ioWsh_5fI20 (Accessed: 10 March 2025).
91 FIFA (2026) Geoff Hurst on famous hat-trick | 1966 FIFA World Cup Final. 29 July. Available at: https://www.youtube.com/watch?v=qxnFW3LjDIg (Accessed: 27 February 2025).
92 Sky Sports Retro (2021) Sir Geoff Hurst on his World Cup Final hat-trick. 11 July. Available at: https://www.youtube.com/watch?v=xZxRFx8IzNU (Accessed: 27 February 2025).
93 Sky Sports Retro (2021) Sir Geoff Hurst on his World Cup Final hat-trick. 11 July. Available at: https://www.youtube.com/watch?v=xZxRFx8IzNU (Accessed: 27 February 2025).
94 Farndale, N. (2001) 'Bruised, battered, but blessed', *Irish Independent*, 28 September.
95 All information about Subbuteo based on Richard Payne, *Fifty Years of Flicking Football* (Harefield: Yore Publications, 1996) and Daniel Tartasky, *Flick to Kick: An Illustrated History of Subbuteo* (2004).
96 Jean Williams, *The History of Women's Football* (Barnsley: Pen & Sword, 2021).
97 Jean Williams, Joanna Compton and Belinda Scarlett, 'Sporting reunions, contemporary collections and collective biographies: a case study of Harry Batt's '71 England Team', in *Upfront and Onside Special Edition: Sport in History*, eds Kay Biscomb, Kath Leflay, Alison Forbes, Tina Smith and Jean Williams (39: 2, June 2019)
98 Jean Williams, *The History of Women's Football*.
99 Ibid.
100 Chris Slegg and Patricia Gregory, *A History of the Women's FA Cup Final* (Cheltenham: The History Press, 2021), p.37. All information on the WFA Cup drawn from this source.
101 For information about Lopez's career, see Sue Lopez, *Women on the Ball: A Guide to the History of Women's Football* (London: Scarlett Press, 1997).
102 The Jack Charlton Tribute Channel (2020) ITV News – Jack Charlton obituary: A look back at a remarkable career and life. 17 July. Available at: https://www.youtube.com/watch?v=CkPgzfSGfrk (Accessed: 25 February 2025).
103 *The Independent* (2023) Bobby Charlton receives lifetime achievement award from brother Jack in resurfaced footage. 22 October. Available at: https://www.dailymotion.com/video/x8pOgpa (Accessed 25 February 2025).
104 Liz Deighan interviewed for the History of the Women's Football Association website, January 2018
105 Deighan, L. (2018) Liz Deighan [Online]. Available at: https://wfahistory.wordpress.com/in-their-own-words/liz-deighan/ (Accessed: 01 March 2025).
106 Deighan, L. (2018) Liz Deighan [Online]. Available at: https://wfahistory.wordpress.com/in-their-own-words/liz-deighan/ (Accessed: 01 March 2025).
107 Unknown author. (2014) Florence 'Flo' Bilton [Online]. Available at: https://womensfootballarchive.org/2014/07/08/administrator-flo-bilton/ (Accessed: 01 March 2025).

108 The Professional Footballers' Association (2022) Viv Anderson: 'There could've been someone before me. We should be telling people these stories'. 25 October. Available at: https://www.youtube.com/watch?v=_Uk-HxsVZH0 (Accessed: 17 February 2025).

109 Speede, R. (2024) To be the first at anything is an unbelievable honour – Anderson. Available at: https://www.bbc.com/sport/football/articles/cqxw94gggeno.amp (Accessed: 17 February 2025).

110 Ibid.

111 Correspondence with Carol Thomas, 30.6.2023.

112 Ibid.

113 Correspondence with Angela Gallimore, 3.7.2023.

114 Correspondence with Carol Thomas, 30.6.2023.

115 Libcom.org (2012) Marching Altogether: Interview with a member of Leeds Fans United Against Racism and Fascism. Available at: https://libcom.org/article/marching-altogether-interview-member-leeds-fans-united-against-racism-and-fascism (Accessed: 17 March 2025).

116 Hartley, G. (2024) Leeds Utd v the National Front. Available at: https://theblizzard.co.uk/leeds-utd-v-the-national-front/featured/ (Accessed: 17 March 2025).

117 Conlon, R. (2017) Leeds United, racism, and the fanzine which forced change at Elland Road. Available at: https://www.planetfootball.com/in-depth/leeds-united-racism-fanzine-forced-change-elland-road (Accessed: 17 March 2025).

118 https://www.liverpoolecho.co.uk/news/liverpool-news/liverpool-believed-us-makes-proud-30739043

119 https://www.britannica.com/event/Hillsborough-disaster

120 https://www.theguardian.com/football/2023/dec/06/hillsborough-disaster-timeline-decades-seeking-justice-and-change.

121 https://www.skysports.com/football/news/11669/12272978/hillsborough-support-group-disbands-as-time-for-families-to-move-on.

122 'A case of have whistle will travel for Gurnam', *Wolverhampton Express and Star*, 17 October 1989.

123 Whitney, A. (2001) 'Referee defeats Football League in race bias case', *Independent*, 6 December.

124 Whitney, A. (2001) 'Referee defeats Football League in race bias case', *Independent*, 6 December.

125 BBC Archive (2024) 1991: JUSTIN FASHANU Interview Wogan (with Clive Anderson) Classic Interviews BBC Archive. 12 November. Available at: https://www.youtube.com/watch?v=R1w_znD09IU (Accessed: 3 February 2025).

126 Sky Sports Premier League (2022) Blackpool's Jake Daniels becomes the first UK male pro footballer in 32 years to come out as gay. 16 May. Available at: https://www.youtube.com/watch?v=-B4ygBi9Bpc (Accessed: 3 February 2025).

127 TV Extra (2015) Paul Gascoigne September 1990. 28 April. Available at: https://www.youtube.com/watch?v=bZRZ48S5Iok (Accessed: 19 February 2025).

128 BBC (2015) Paul Gascoigne: I was glad when told I was an alcoholic. Available at: https://www.bbc.co.uk/sport/football/33051499 (Accessed: 19 February 2025).

129 Deane, B. (2022) 'National Football Museum: Brian Deane'. Interview by Marek Romaniszyn [in person], 1 August.

130 Sky Sports Retro (2022) Brian Deane reflects on scoring the first Premier League goal. 15 August. Available at: https://www.youtube.com/watch?v=emEd2pJkogI (Accessed: 8 March 2025).
131 Sky Sports Retro (2022) Brian Deane reflects on scoring the first Premier League goal. 15 August. Available at: https://www.youtube.com/watch?v=emEd2pJkogI (Accessed: 8 March 2025).
132 John Watt's handwritten notes donated to the National Football Museum.
133 Willars, I. (1992) 'Sky wars move to court', Sports Argus, 23 May, 1.
134 Sky Sports News (2023) LGBT+ History Month: Hackney Women FC - Europe's first openly gay women's football team. 27 February. Available at: https://www.youtube.com/watch?v=GHYyj7sj3XA (Accessed: 12 March 2025).
135 Ibid.
136 Adobe Women's FA Cup (2024) Behind The Badge | Hackney WFC | Cup Stories | Adobe Women's FA Cup. 23 December. Available at: https://www.youtube.com/watch?v=77qRzUN14OA (Accessed: 12 March 2025).
137 BBC Sport (2022) Goals, celebrations & Germany's missing number 9: Jurgen Klinsmann Q&A BBC Sport. 27 November. Available at: https://www.youtube.com/watch?v=aX1lSBE1u18 (Accessed: 3 February 2025).
138 BBC Sport (2022) Goals, celebrations & Germany's missing number 9: Jurgen Klinsmann Q&A BBC Sport. 27 November. Available at: https://www.youtube.com/watch?v=aX1lSBE1u18 (Accessed: 3 February 2025).
139 Tottenham Hostpur (2023) 25 years ago today | Jurgen's four goals against Wimbledon. Available at: https://www.tottenhamhotspur.com/news/2023/may/25-years-ago-today-jurgen-klinsmanns-four-goals-against-wimbledon/ (Accessed: 3 February 2025).
140 Sky Sports Premier League (2024) The Ian Wright Story FULL Monday Night Football Interview. 12 March. Available at: https://www.youtube.com/watch?v=h5B0hihEPhs (Accessed: 13 February 2025).
141 ITV Sport (2024) Ian Wright on his early experiences in football Black History Month. 8 October. Available at: https://www.youtube.com/watch?v=Dkk9Glw8RkI (Accessed: 13 February 2025).
142 Sky Sports Premier League (2024) The Ian Wright Story FULL Monday Night Football Interview. 12 March. Available at: https://www.youtube.com/watch?v=h5B0hihEPhs (Accessed: 13 February 2025).
143 West Bromwich Albion (2015) Frank Skinner talks about his friendship with Jeff Astle. 8 April. Available at: https://www.youtube.com/watch?v=9T-xlH1w7yk (Accessed: 4 March 2025).
144 AbsoluteLee Podcast (2022) Jason Lee & David Baddiel Discuss Fantasy Football Blackface Sketches AbsoluteLee Podcast Ep. 01. 21 November. Available at: https://www.youtube.com/watch?v=he6Nq2lWLJ0 (Accessed: 4 March 2025).
145 West Bromwich Albion (2015) Frank Skinner talks about his friendship with Jeff Astle. 8 April. Available at: https://www.youtube.com/watch?v=9T-xlH1w7yk (Accessed: 4 March 2025).
146 All information about Chris Unger is drawn from https://unlockingthehiddenhistory.wordpress.com/2018/01/09/learning-more-about-womens-football-collector-chris-unger/ (Accessed: 14 February 2025).
147 Ibid.
148 https://www.youtube.com/watch?v=g8E0s6hnAvk (Accessed: 7 March 2025).
149 Ibid.

150 All information based onhttps://www.youtube.com/watch?v=g8E0s6hnAvk and, https://www.pcgamer.com/the-history-of-championship-manager-and-football-manager/ (Accessed 7 March 2025).

151 https://www.fourfourtwo.com/features/football-manager-the-greatest-cult-heroes-of-all-time (Accessed: 27 February 2025).

152 https://www.theguardian.com/football/2017/sep/22/championship-manager-game-football-25-years (Accessed: 27 February 2025).

153 Sky Sports Retro (2022) 'Nothing to do with me!' – Robbie Fowler on Liverpool's infamous white FA Cup suits. 14 May. Available at: https://www.youtube.com/watch?v=rWqbbRSK6T4 (Accessed: 14 February 2025).

154 Sky Sports Retro (2022) 'Nothing to do with me!' – Robbie Fowler on Liverpool's infamous white FA Cup suits. 14 May. Available at: https://www.youtube.com/watch?v=rWqbbRSK6T4 (Accessed: 14 February 2025).

155 Sky Sports Retro (2022) 'Nothing to do with me!' – Robbie Fowler on Liverpool's infamous white FA Cup suits. 14 May. Available at: https://www.youtube.com/watch?v=rWqbbRSK6T4 (Accessed: 14 February 2025).

156 'Who is this star?', *Sunderland Daily Echo*, 6 March 2000

157 Lavelle, P. (2000) 'David faces up to West End role!' *Shields Gazette*, 9 March.

158 'Middlesbrough fanzine *Fly Me To The Moon* overcame many challenges to celebrate 35 years', *Teesside Live*, 22 November 2023

159 Johns, C. (2023) Middlesbrough fanzine Fly Me To The Moon overcame many challenges to celebrate 35 years [Online]. Available at: https://www.gazettelive.co.uk/sport/football/football-news/middlesbrough-fanzine-fly-moon-overcame-28149576 (Accessed: 01 March 2025).

160 O'Connor, S. (2023) 'It was a blur' – Denis Irwin on United's 10 days of treble glory and whether City can match it. Available at: https://www.independent.ie/sport/soccer/it-was-a-blur-denis-irwin-on-uniteds-10-days-of-treble-glory-and-whether-city-can-match-it/a1892892783.html (Accessed: 3 February 2025).

161 Mitten, A. (2021) FFT meets Denis Irwin: 'Nothing can top the 1999 Manchester United team – but our '94 side was such a joy to play in'. Available at: https://www.fourfourtwo.com/features/fft-meets-denis-irwin-nothing-can-top-1999-but-our-94-side-was-such-a-joy-to-play-in (Accessed: 3 February 2025).

162 https://www.fourfourtwo.com/features/fantasy-premier-league-the-crazy-history-and-inside-story-of-the-rise-of-fpl (Accessed: 25 February 2025).

163 Ibid.

164 Ibid.

165 For this and all the ITV Digital adverts involving Monkey, see https://www.youtube.com/watch?v=jawUyxqgJtA (Accessed: 24 February 2025).

166 https://www.fourfourtwo.com/features/everyone-said-this-sounds-too-good-to-be-true-it-turned-out-to-be-exactly-that-remembering-the-fall-of-itv-digital-twenty-years-on (Accessed 24 February 2025).

167 Ibid.

168 https://www.theguardian.com/media/2002/aug/05/marketingandpr.advertising (Accessed: 24 February 2025).

169 http://news.bbc.co.uk/sportacademy/hi/sa/football/disability/newsid_2079000/2079661.stm.

170 England (2024) Fara Williams On Scoring on Lionesses Debut, The Fara Williams Pitch and Lionesses Euro Win! 25 July. Available at: https://www.youtube.com/watch?v=zruaXp9nllc (Accessed: 13 March 2025).

171 Lobb, A. (2023) Fara Williams: 'I was living in hostels for seven years – football saved me'. Available at: https://www.bigissue.com/culture/fara-williams-i-was-living-in-hostels-for-seven-years-football-saved-me/ (Accessed: 13 March 2025).

172 Ibid.

173 Football Association (2020) Lionesses centurion and FA WSL legend Eni Aluko has announced her retirement. Available at: https://www.thefa.com/news/2020/jan/15/eni-aluko-announces-retirement-150120 (Accessed: 25 February 2025).

174 Women In The World (2015) Eni Aluko on being a trailblazer for female athletes. 13 October. Available at: https://www.youtube.com/watch?v=j-wPHDEWx3c (Accessed: 25 February 2025).

175 Sky Sports (2022) Eni Aluko: We must open talent pool as wide as possible. Available at: https://www.skysports.com/watch/video/sports/12726131/eni-aluko-we-must-open-talent-pool-as-wide-as-possible (Accessed: 25 February 2025).

176 Coaches' Voice (2017) Being First Hope Powell England Women, 1998–2013. Available at: https://learning.coachesvoice.com/being-first/ (Accessed: 28 February).

177 BBC (2009) Powell proud despite losing final. Available at: http://news.bbc.co.uk/sport1/hi/football/women/8249632.stm (Accessed: 28 February).

178 Brighton & Hove Albion FC (2022) Hope Powell on Euros Success And New WSL Season. 6 August. Available at: https://www.youtube.com/watch?v=MoVStNcookQ (Accessed: 28 February 2025).

179 https://www.theguardian.com/football/2010/feb/10/amy-fearn-female-league-referee (Accessed: 26 February 2025).

180 Ibid.

181 Information on the history of female referees from https://nationalfootballmuseum.com/stories/female-referees-england/ (Accessed: 26 February 2025).

182 The Football Referee, November 1994, p.12. The official was unnamed in a letter of complaint sent to the editor.

183 http://news.bbc.co.uk/sport1/hi/football/6142974.stm (Accessed: 26 February 2025).

184 https://www.bbc.co.uk/news/uk-england-derbyshire-65904820 (Accessed: 26 February 2025).

185 'Last action heroes engulfed by words', *Birmingham Daily Post*, 11 December 1999.

186 Unknown author. (2001) 'Motty collects gong', *Halifax Evening Courier*, 28 November.

187 https://www.thefa.com/about-football-association/for-casey

188 Ibid.

189 Stead, Emily, *Changing the Game with Casey Stoney*, Studio Press: 2019.

190 Ibid.

191 Sky Sports (2023) National Inclusion Week: Ex-footballer Alistair Patrick-Heselton wants young players to discuss mental health. Available at: https://www.skysports.com/football/news/11095/12969907/national-inclusion-week-alistair-patrick-heselton-wants-mental-health-conversations-to-become-the-norm-among-aspiring-young-footballers (Accessed: 21 March 2025).
Professional Footballers' Association (2012) Patrick-Heselton aiming for Paralympic glory. Available at: https://www.thepfa.com/news/2012/8/28/going-for-gold (Accessed: 21 March 2025).

192 Ibid.
193 Inspiration Athletes, Alistair Patrick-Heselton: A promising footballer who went on to represent Team GB at the Paralympic Games (Accessed: 8 July 2025) https://inspirationalathletes.co.uk/athletes/alistair-patrick-heselton-2/#testimonial
194 Conn, D. (2012) Defeat and chants tarnish Liverpool's celebration of justice [Online]. Available at: https://www.theguardian.com/football/2012/sep/23/liverpool-manchester-united-hillsborough-munich (Accessed: 01 March 2025).
195 Ibid.
196 https://www.bbc.co.uk/sport/football/28642187 (Accessed: 16 January 2025).
197 https://www.bbc.co.uk/sport/football/articles/c7891el384vo (Accessed: 16 January 2025).
198 'Former captain of England partially-sighted futsal team Daley recognised in Queen's birthday honours', Insidethegames.biz, 10 October 2020
199 Beaney, A. (2020) Captain of blind futsal announces retirement [Online]. Available at: https://www.blogpreston.co.uk/2020/03/captain-of-englands-blind-futsal-announces-retirement/ (Accessed: 01 March 2025).
200 All quotes for this object from Clark, L. (2023) 'National Football Museum: Lucy Clark'. Interview by Marek Romaniszyn [in person], 30 May.
201 Ibid.
202 Ibid
203 https://www.bbc.co.uk/sport/av/football/46652795 (Accessed: 11 March 2025).
204 https://www.theguardian.com/football/2018/jul/10/psychology-england-football-team-change-your-life-pippa-grange (Accessed: 11 March 2025).
205 https://www.bbc.co.uk/sport/football/45886746 (Accessed: 17 January 2025).
206 https://www.tiktok.com/@england/video/6981538742301396229?lang=en (Accessed: 11 March 2025).
207 Hope Powell interview with NFM 2019.
208 https://www.theguardian.com/sport/2024/dec/31/crazy-stories-hunt-every-sports-statue-world (Accessed: 10.3.2025).
209 Hope Powell interview with NFM 2019.
210 Amelie Waine and Scarlett Latta interviews with NFM 2019.
211 Fleur Cousens interview with NFM 2019.
212 https://www.skysports.com/football/news/11667/12007883/marcus-rashford-boris-johnson-congratulates-man-utd-striker-over-free-school-meals-campaign.
213 https://www.independent.co.uk/sport/football/premier-league/trent-alexander-arnold-black-lives-matter-liverpool-everton-derby-a9577811.html.
214 All quotes for this object from Houghton, S. (2023) 'National Football Museum: Steph Houghton'. Interview by Marek Romaniszyn [in person], 15 February.
215 Oral History Interview with Daniel Hamilton, 30 July 2021.
216 https://www.theguardian.com/football/2021/apr/24/the-week-english-football-fans-bit-back-against-super-league-the-billionaire-owners (Accessed: 14 March 2025).
217 https://www.youtube.com/watch?v=n0Ou7KzuUck (Accessed: 14 March 2025).
218 PA Sport Staff (2021) England captain Harry Kane to wear rainbow armband against Germany. Available at: https://www.independent.co.uk/sport/football/harry-kane-manuel-neuer-england-germany-uefa-b1874400.html (Accessed: 14 February 2025).
219 Ibid.

220 Oral History Interview with Barry Lenton, 8 February 2021, NFM Collections.
221 Oral History Interview with Richard Cross, 3 March 2021, NFM Collections.
222 https://www.dailymail.co.uk/sport/sportsnews/article-11198543/The-game-right-foot-ball-one-weekend-without-football-not-ask-for.html.
223 https://www.dailymail.co.uk/sport/football/article-11198581/Its-crazy-football-fans-denied-chance-pay-respects-Queen.html.
224 Tranmere Rovers v Bradford City, 13.9.2022
225 BBC (2022) Ellen White: Manchester City and England striker announces retirement. Available at: https://www.bbc.co.uk/sport/football/62636434 (Accessed: 6 February 2025).
226 BBC Sounds (2022) Ellen White on winning Euro 2022: 'The most special moment ever'. 27 October. Available at: https://www.youtube.com/watch?v=fYqtEpU3tdc (Accessed: 6 February 2025).
227 BBC (2022) Ellen White: Manchester City and England striker announces retirement. Available at: https://www.bbc.co.uk/sport/football/62636434 (Accessed: 6 February 2025).
228 Davis, K. (2024) Text conversation with Nikita Parris, 28 August.
229 Romaniszyn, M (2023) Teams call conversation with Nikita Parris, 2 November.
230 Davis, K. (2024) Text conversation with Nikita Parris, 28 August.
231 Wilkes, L. (2023) EXCLUSIVE: FIFA Best winner Mary Earps discusses the moment she wanted to become a goalkeeper. Available at: https://www.nottinghampost.com/sport/football/football-news/mary-earps-fifa-best-goalkeeper-8195967 (Accessed: 11 February 2025).
232 Summerfield, J. (2024) Mary Earps wins 2023 The Best FIFA Women's Goalkeeper award. Available at: https://www.90min.com/posts/mary-earps-wins-2023-best-fifa-womens-goalkeeper-award#:~:text=Manchester%20United%20and%20England%20goalkeeper%20Mary%20Earps%20has,beating%20fellow%20nominees%20Mackenzie%20Arnold%20and%20Catalina%20Coll (Accessed: 11 February 2025).
233 Firth, M. (2023) Man Utd's Mary Earps crowned FIFA's Best Goalkeeper after self-doubt nearly made her quit. Available at: https://www.mancunianmatters.co.uk/sport/02032023-man-utds-mary-earps-crowned-fifas-best-goalkeeper-after-self-doubt-nearly-made-her-quit/ (Accessed: 11 February 2025).
234 ITV Sport (2023) Nobody in this team shies away! – Leah Williamson and England react to #Finalissima win ITV Sport. 6 April. Available at: https://www.youtube.com/watch?v=epqqKrL41ao (Accessed: 18 February 2025).
235 BBC Sport (2023) New England kit for Women's World Cup has blue shorts because of period concerns. Available at: https://www.bbc.co.uk/sport/football/65160447 (Accessed: 18 February 2025).
236 ITV Sport (2023) Nobody in this team shies away! – Leah Williamson and England react to #Finalissima win ITV Sport. 6 April. Available at: https://www.youtube.com/watch?v=epqqKrL41ao (Accessed: 18 February 2025).
237 Jamie Jackson, 'A Twist in the Tale', *Guardian*, 23 April 2006, https://www.theguardian.com/football/2006/apr/23/newsstory.sport1.
238 Cuthbert, E., 'National Football Museum: Erin Cuthbert', interview by Marek Romaniszyn, 8 August 2022
239 De Cordova-Reid, B. 'National Football Museum: Bobby De Cordova-Reid', interview by Marek Romaniszyn, 11 May 2023.

HarperNorth
Windmill Green
24 Mount Street
Manchester M2 3NX

A division of
HarperCollins*Publishers*
1 London Bridge Street
London SE1 9GF

www.harpercollins.co.uk

HarperCollins*Publishers*
Macken House, 39/40 Mayor Street Upper
Dublin 1, D01 C9W8, Ireland

First published by HarperCollins*Publishers* 2025

1 3 5 7 9 10 8 6 4 2

© National Football Museum 2025

National Football Museum asserts the moral right to be identified as the author of this work

A catalogue record of this book is available from the British Library

HB ISBN 978-0-00-872914-1

Printed and bound by PNB Print, Latvia

All rights reserved. No part of this publication may be reproduced, stored in a retrieval system, or transmitted, in any form or by any means, electronic, mechanical, photocopying, recording or otherwise, without the prior written permission of the publishers.

Without limiting the exclusive rights of any author, contributor or the publisher of this publication, any unauthorised use of this publication to train generative artificial Intelligence (AI) technologies is expressly prohibited. HarperCollins also exercise their rights under Article 4(3) of the Digital Single Market Directive 2019/790 and expressly reserve this publication from the text and data mining exception.

This book is produced from independently certified FSC™ paper
to ensure responsible forest management.

For more information visit: www.harpercollins.co.uk/green

For more information visit: www.harpercollins.co.uk/green